INKED
THE SKY IS THE LIMIT

Unmukt Chand was born on 26 March 1993 in Delhi. He traces his roots to Pithoragarh, Uttarakhand. The promising cricketer, who led the India Under-19 team to World Cup victory in Australia in August 2012, has also captained the India A one-day team. Apart from representing India A, Unmukt is also part of India Under-23, North Zone, Delhi, and Delhi Daredevils teams. At age seventeen, he was the youngest to play the Indian Premier League. The prolific batsman also led the India U-19 side to victory in the Asia Cup (2012), and two U-19 quadrangular series (2011 and 2012).

Among the prominent awards that have come his way in his cricketing career are the Castrol Best Junior Cricketer of the Year 2011–2012, and the CEAT Indian Youngster of the Year 2012.

Unmukt is an avid reader and maintains a regular diary and, much like he collects his runs, is forever adding to his English vocabulary. He is presently doing his undergraduation at St. Stephen's College, Delhi.

T0290279

The Sky Is the Limit

My Journey to
the World Cup

UNMUKT
CHAND

With a Foreword by
Sir Vivian Richards

PENGUIN

INKED
Published by the Penguin Group
Penguin Books India Pvt. Ltd, 11 Community Centre, Panchsheel Park,
New Delhi 110 017, India
Penguin Group (USA) Inc., 375 Hudson Street, New York, New York 10014, USA
Penguin Group (Canada), 90 Eglinton Avenue East, Suite 700, Toronto, Ontario,
M4P 2Y3, Canada (a division of Pearson Penguin Canada Inc.)
Penguin Books Ltd, 80 Strand, London WC2R 0RL, England
Penguin Ireland, 25 St Stephen's Green, Dublin 2, Ireland (a division of Penguin
Books Ltd)
Penguin Group (Australia), 707 Collins Street, Melbourne, Victoria 3008, Australia
(a division of Pearson Australia Group Pty Ltd)
Penguin Group (NZ), 67 Apollo Drive, Rosedale, Auckland 0632, New Zealand
(a division of Pearson New Zealand Ltd)
Penguin Group (South Africa) (Pty) Ltd, Block D, Rosebank Office Park, 181 Jan
Smuts Avenue, Parktown North, Johannesburg 2193, South Africa

Penguin Books Ltd, Registered Offices: 80 Strand, London WC2R 0RL, England

First published in Inked by Penguin Books India 2013

Copyright © Unmukt Chand 2013

All rights reserved

10 9 8 7 6 5 4 3 2 1

The views and opinions expressed in this book are the author's own and the facts
are as reported by him which have been verified to the extent possible, and the
publishers are not in any way liable for the same.

ISBN 9780143333074

Typeset in Garamond Regular by SÜRYA, New Delhi

This book is sold subject to the condition that it shall not, by way of trade or
otherwise, be lent, resold, hired out, or otherwise circulated without the publisher's
prior written consent in any form of binding or cover other than that in which it is
published and without a similar condition including this condition being imposed
on the subsequent purchaser and without limiting the rights under copyright
reserved above, no part of this publication may be reproduced, stored in or
introduced into a retrieval system, or transmitted in any form or by any means
(electronic, mechanical, photocopying, recording or otherwise), without the prior
written permission of both the copyright owner and the above-mentioned publisher
of this book.

To my teammates and support staff
who helped India win the Under-19 World Cup.

And to the most stimulating word in the English language,
one that has urged mankind to scale newer heights:
BELIEVE!

Contents

Foreword

When I first saw Unmukt Chand in the Under-19 World Cup, it was in Australia and I was immediately impressed with his mannerism at the crease. It was then that I recognized that at such an early age, he looked the part, and right away I took a liking to him as a batsman. India won that World Cup, so it is my belief if he continues to demonstrate the toughness and good form he has displayed at such an early age, it can only result in good things for Indian cricket's future.

Having the opportunity to work with Delhi Daredevils, I was even more impressed when I discovered that he was part of the team. He was a keen student with a lot of energy and enthusiasm, always seeking the knowledge and the art of how to improve his game. I would like to offer these words of advice to him: 'Keep learning every day and never ever adopt the attitude that you know it all.'

I do hope that anyone who has the opportunity to read this book will find it interesting, especially to discover his enthusiasm and zest to always try and better his game. The reader will be captivated by his achievements and this should be an insight to what more can be attained in the future.

Unmukt, I wish you lots of good luck going forward!

Viv
(Sir Vivian Richards)

Note from V.V.S. Laxman

I would like to congratulate you on your first book. The title, *The Sky Is the Limit*, is very apt and that is exactly what I see in your future. It was a delight to watch the way you and your team played in Australia to win the Under-19 World Cup in 2012, and the entire country is proud of your achievement. The thought of writing this book and sharing your journey from childhood to the hour of your World Cup triumph shows what a mature individual you are. I really enjoyed reading the book, especially the way you describe your teammates and the coaching staff. The way it portrays the various aspects of junior cricket is really enlightening. This is a good read and I would recommend all aspiring cricketers to read it and get inspired. ALL THE BEST IN YOUR CAREER!

V.V.S Laxman

Introduction

The harder you work, the harder it is to surrender.

—Vince Lombardi

Settling back in my chair in the pavilion of the Tony Ireland Stadium, in Townsville, Queensland, I caught my breath and reached for my BlackBerry. We had just won a closely fought quarter-final against Pakistan. I updated my BBM status: 'I can already feel d cup in my hands.' Six days later, the Indian Under-19 cricket team defeated the Australian Under-19 team to win the World Cup.

Despite struggling in the tournament at the beginning—and even in the final—we managed to achieve the ultimate goal of every junior cricketer. Of course, we managed to do it only because of the hard work put in by the team and its support staff. All the effort invested in preparing for the tournament had built within us a self-belief that gave us a 'never-let-go' attitude, and nothing could stop us. The match against Pakistan was a roller-coaster ride. We got them out cheaply, and then we collapsed losing the first three wickets (starting with mine) for just eight runs. We recovered and staged another collapse just before the finish, this time losing three wickets for three runs. But the last two batsmen played heroically taking seven overs to score ten runs! Once we won that match I had no doubt: we were going to win the World Cup.

The idea of writing down my journey to the World Cup came to me about three months before the tournament. I did not know then that we would win but the very deal of putting everything down on paper was thrilling—I could write down my thoughts, about the team's preparation and related things, especially on the assumption that we were going to win. I realized that writing things down would help me in other ways too. I did not want the pressure of the tournament to get to me, and writing was a good way to remain engaged with the game while giving myself a little space for detachment. Believe me when I say that a lot of what you will read was first written while I was still at the preparatory camp hosted by the

National Cricket Academy in Bangalore, three months before the tournament started.

But when did this journey actually start? It is difficult for me to pin down the exact time. Technically, it would be the quadrangular series in Vizag held between 27 September–8 October 2011, the first international tournament specially organized by the BCCI to prepare the team for the World Cup. But at an individual level, for me and many others before me, the journey had begun much earlier.

You cannot become a good sportsman in a year. In any sport, it requires years of hard work and practice to sharpen your skills and become someone worth reckoning. In my case I can say that my journey began when I chose cricket over everything else in my life— when I was all of four years old. So before I tell you about the actual journey to the World Cup, I would like to take you through the journey which brought me to the Under-19 level. I talk about my experiences at the Under-19 level, at the IPL (Indian Premier League) and the Asia Cup. I share stories about the people who helped me along the way. I recount details about the preparation and the story of the final victory in Australia.

It is a significant journey, though hopefully not my only one. I first wrote this story primarily for myself, but I think it might interest others. It may inspire some to focus energies at an early age and, more importantly, it may encourage others to support young people when they try to live their dreams. And some of you might just like to know where I came from and what I did along the way.

PART I

FOR THE LOVE OF THE GAME

1

The Early Days

Adversity causes some men to break;
others to break records.

—William Arthur Ward

I have heard people say that 'passion' drove them to pursue their hobbies, that it was their first love, etc. I can't help but think that that's 'too much'. You cannot associate a word as strong as 'passion' with such things, especially once you are an adult. When I was a kid, it so happened that I loved holding the bat in my hands and hitting the ball as far as I could. It was fun. At that point I had no aim, no goal, no ambitions. I was just crazy about cricket. This game, above all the things that a four-year-old does, gave me a special

3

happiness. That was passion. It was pure; it was innocent; it was a time when I played for the sheer love I had for the game. Now when I look back at those days, I feel like my passion, while it is still there, has been diluted by the things that come with adult life. Now I have to worry about my team, my personal performance, letting the country down, figuring out strategy as a captain and a hundred other things, and sometimes it's hard to find that core of passion that I began with.

I can't really remember the day I first held a bat in my hands, but I vividly remember the early days when I woke everyone up in the wee hours and pushed them out of bed to take me for practice in a nearby ground. Luckily, my dad and uncle were more passionate about cricket than I was. They were always eager to make me practise. My uncle has contributed the most to making me a cricketer, honing my skills in the sport and in many other areas. Today I believe that to be successful, one needs a good mentor. My uncle has been more than a mentor to me; he has been a true friend. I have spent so much time with him and have been so influenced by him that I have become his alter ego—our bonding is beyond definition. I have been very lucky to have had his presence in my life. I have also been very lucky in the support my parents have given me. I have always been their first priority. They would sacrifice anything for me. They have been like a beacon leading me forward. I could not have gone astray in their presence. They raised me on the plank of a strong set of values, which is why I have a balanced outlook on life. They have done their best to make me strong and steadfast so that I would make my way through life without much faltering.

With all this support, every morning I'd be at the park near my house, bright and early. This park had once been in a shambles. My father and uncle worked on the ground and prepared a nice-looking pitch. The two cricket crazies would bowl at me—papa was a real fast bowler and chacha tried his off and leg spin on me. Chacha had just left the army so he had his own parameters for physical fitness: he made me run long distances even at that very young age, and tested my endurance all the time. One summer, he convinced papa that I should be able to sustain three to four hours of practice under the hot sun. So there I was at the park at noon in the hottest month of the year, sweating and battling it out.

We went to that park almost every day, full of excitement. Once we were there, the first activity was running. Uncle would run with me while papa prepared the pitch and set up the stumps. The park was full of clusters of dense bushes, and the ball would invariably head straight into them. To make things worse, the bushes were used by people as toilets, and they stank horribly—but this did not deter my trainers who often had to fetch the ball from deep inside them. Their dedication often overwhelmed me. They were very particular that I polish all the skills I would need as a cricketer. So, once the batting was over, I had to practise ground fielding, running between the wickets and different types of catching, and then I used to bowl at them.

They were committed to making sure I could handle the reality of international cricket. I remember vividly that once, when papa was bowling quick with a leather ball on an underprepared wicket, the ball rose sharply from the good-length spot and crashed into my helmet. A stream of blood trickled out of my nose. They asked me if I could continue and I said yes—because I knew that deep in their hearts neither of them wanted to leave the ground.

I started to receive formal coaching in cricket even before I turned eight. Before that I had to undergo a proper test conducted at the National Stadium, New Delhi, by M.P. Singh sir. He is one of the senior cricket coaches at the National Stadium, which is under the Sports Authority of India (SAI). And he happened to be my first coach. It was the best place for budding cricketers at that time. I remember that, for nearly two whole years, I just did one drill: backward/forward defence and drive. I will always hold M.P. Singh sir in high regard for the solid foundation he gave me. I have been very lucky that way—I've always found the right people at the right place and at the right time.

I met Bishen Singh Bedi sir at an early age—twelve. Bedi sir used to select talented boys and conduct a month-long summer camp. This time it was held at Dharamsala. It was the first time I'd travelled without my family, and the camp gave me a lot of confidence. Bedi sir also convinced my parents of my potential, and appreciated that they had inculcated good values in me. My habit of diary writing came in handy for me at the camp because Bedi sir wanted all of us to write daily diaries based on the day's activities. He used to check the diary next day and comment on it. He was very impressed with my diary-writing skills and told me to continue this habit. The next year, 2006, he took me to Sydney with his senior club team where I played a few matches and had my first taste of batting on those bouncy pitches. I still talk to him whenever I have doubts. I have always been enriched and enlightened by his broad ideas and thoughts on cricket and its history. He convinced my parents that hard work, sincerity, family values, a cool head and a down-to-earth approach would take me further.

The next turning point came when I was in class IX. While I continued with cricket coaching, I took an important decision that turned out to be really fruitful: I changed schools from DPS, Noida, to Modern School, Barakhamba Road, in class IX. It was a tough decision. I had studied in DPS from the beginning, and by then had developed close relationships with many classmates. But the passion (yes, at that point it could be called a 'passion') for cricket made me bold enough to change schools. School cricket is very important ; it gives you the right exposure making you participate in many tournaments. Because I was at DPS in Noida, I had been unable to play in the major Delhi tournaments. So we decided to shift my base to Modern School, which was at that time considered one of the best places for cricket and other sports, along with studies.

It wasn't easy to get admission to Modern School. They conducted a written test and interviewed me and my parents. And it so happened that it wasn't cricket that helped me make the cut—it was my good academic record and swimming achievements (I had won a bronze medal in a national-level school contest) that got me in. It was at this school that I began to understand what competitive cricket was really all about. I started playing with senior players about whom I had heard plenty. Many of them represented Delhi state in different age groups. I remember the first time I went to Modern School for practice. I was very nervous; my hands were trembling with anxiety. That was the first day. But over time, I relaxed and became proud to be a part of the group. My coaches at Modern School, Navin Chopra sir and Uday Gupte sir hold a special place in my heart. Chopra sir is one of those coaches who try to help in every possible way. He used to make sure I didn't have any trouble with the attendance and exams; he, along with Uday sir, helped me get a fee concession that made my life much easier. Once I left school and moved to college, I understood that life wasn't that easy. I really appreciate how much he took care of me in a way that would never happen again.

The four years at Modern School were very productive and filled with fun. The school gave me the confidence that I lacked before—I began to believe in myself. It also gave me the right attitude, the so-called 'Modernite' attitude. I feel that personality development is very important for cricketers. They meet so many people from different backgrounds and need to know how to conduct themselves among these people. Modern School taught me that valuable lesson.

The other important thing about Modern School was academics. I somehow always managed to pay the utmost attention to academics—maybe because my parents never let me compromise. Most of the guys who played cricket used to bunk classes even when they were not playing matches, but I never did that. I was very fond of psychology (one of the subjects I studied in school). I attended all the psychology classes and even chose to sit in other psychology sections whenever I was free. They say that when the going gets tough, the tough get going. It has always happened with me. I perform best under tough conditions. I love challenges. I took mathematics as one of the subjects in classes XI and XII, knowing that I would have to burn the midnight oil to get decent marks. But I did it anyway. I thought cricket would go well with mathematics. Maths would help me tactically, statistically—working with the angles and stuff like that. I never blamed one thing for another. People always looked at me like I was crazy—it's rare for a cricketer to mix a difficult subject like mathematics with their game, but somehow I felt like I needed the challenge. I have always wanted to push the boundaries. I think there are different perspectives to a situation. There is always a relationship between two things, a relationship that is sometimes difficult to see, but it exists. Somehow I believe in this relationship and it has done wonders for me. I have always surprised my teachers and classmates with my marks. Even today I make time to study, which is why I scored well in the first semester of my BA programme at St. Stephen's College. I can never give up studying—I plan to continue even if I play for the national side.

The next turning point of my life came when I joined the LB Shastri Cricket Club at Bharat Nagar under Sanjay Bhardwaj sir (who also coaches Gautam Gambhir and Amit Mishra). The National Stadium had been closed for renovation for the Commonwealth Games, and I had to look for a new place to practise. Bhardwaj sir is a Level-3 coach. He is very passionate about coaching, and a great human being. I like to think of him as a walking encyclopedia of cricket. Whenever I have asked about a problem, psychological or technical, he has always given me a satisfactory solution. He is a humble person and I am fortunate to have a coach and mentor like him in my life. I respect his dedication to the boys who live there and train. To

30/5/85 . B·B·CC·T

3rd day.

And now, the third day of the B.B.C.C.T was as exciting as both the days. So I woke up early in the morning and did toilet and then dressed in my casuals. We left the resort at 7:40 a.m and reached the ground after 20 minutes. As we reached the ground we started with fitness. First we did yoga then specially Anilom Vilonm and then ran for half an hour. After that Jatin Bhaiya made us do some very difficult drills. But there managed to do that. With this the fitness session finished. We were served with our breakfast after that. It was a delicious food. They gave us milk with conflakes, bread butter, & boiled egg. We ate the food and then Shashi Bhaiya called us for fielding. I was satisfied with my fielding but I missed two catches which would shouldn't have been caught easily. But But After some time we were served with our

**Diary written while attending
Bishan Singh Bedi's camp at Dharamsala**

lunch. I liked the food very much. We were given chicken, chapatees, pulse etc. I ate a lot. After that I went to sleep. I woke up at 4:40.

1 am Then the net session took place. Sunny, Yudhvir, Vishwas, Ishmeet Neil and me went to Rajdeep sir was for batting practice. He made us do fundamentals. I did it properly I think I did it properly. After this we did a lit bit conditioning. Then went for tea. Aft After this Bedie sir gave us the lecture. After this Nhr we had our dinner. Then we went to the resort in the samo. We slept the as early as possible as we reached the resort.

V. Good.
Keep it up.
Your written will help
express on with your
another learning habit
make diary a habit
writing.
31/5/05

him the ground is his home and the students are his family.

To succeed in most sports you need more than proper training and guidance; you need good equipment too. Cricket is an expensive game. You need to invest a lot of money when you start playing professionally. Just a good bat costs about Rs 10,000 to 20,000. Initially, I played with normal bats bought from neighbourhood sports shops. Later, I went all the way to Meerut to buy some cheap, good, discounted bats. I loved my bats so much that I would not throw them away even after they were broken. I used to have them repaired so many times that the whole blade of the bats would be covered with gut (the fibre used to repair bats). There were some that were my absolute favourites because I had scored a lot of runs using them. I used those bats till their wood fell apart. I did this also because I could not afford to buy new bats every month. My parents had a modest income and they were doing their bit by giving me a good education. It was a tough time for them.

However, I was very fortunate that I received assistance at every stage of my journey, even financially. DPS, Noida, awarded me full fee concessions in classes VII and VIII. My school cricket coach Sumit Dogra sir was instrumental in this, speaking to the principal to get me the concession. In Modern School too, I had to pay only half the fees in classes XI and XII. Here again my coaches Navin Chopra sir and Uday Gupte sir played key roles in getting the concession. My Australian tour was sponsored by a number of my father's friends and colleagues. But the biggest financial support that actually relieved my parents of some of their burden came from Mr Vikram Thapar, chairman and MD of the IM Thapar group. He sponsored a stipend of Rs 5000 per month for five years starting when I was fourteen. He also sponsored my Under-19 England tour in the year 2009. This happened because Sudha Ramanathan, who lives in our neighbourhood and works with that group, was kind enough to intervene on my behalf. The management of Medha Apartment, where I live, gave me special permission to use the vacant space in its basement for practising with wet Cosco balls. This happened after playing for Delhi Under-15 when I realized that I needed more practice hours to survive in competitive cricket. Those long hours of practice really helped me in toning up my batting skills, and I still utilize that space. It was interesting to know that the people of my apartment watched the U-19 final live on a big screen put up in the same basement.

Money plays a crucial role in the life of a sportsperson, and it is not an easy hurdle to overcome. I had tried to get contracts from various sports equipment companies but only managed to land one after playing Ranji for Delhi.

These were the major stops on that vital part of my journey in those early days. While I received support from various people in various spheres of my life, there were the crucial decisions that were taken about coaches and schooling. Then of course, there was the hard work I put in, and the ways I found to motivate myself.

2

My Stint with NCA

You always have more time than you think you do.

—R. Sridhar, Fielding Coach, NCA, Bengaluru

Be it any field, the training centres play a special role. This is especially so when it comes to sports. They are essentially the place where your skills are honed to perfection and you become the absolute best you can be. For Indian cricketers, this happens at the National Cricket Academy (NCA), Bengaluru, which plays the pre-eminent role in training and rehabilitation.

After playing for Delhi at the Under-15 level, I realized that I needed a specialized kind of training regime to keep myself in the race for competitive cricket, and I was told that I would get it at the NCA.

The only way to get there was to excel at the state level and then get into the Zonal Cricket Academy (ZCA, North Zone) from where the best players are sent to the NCA for a month-long camp. Of course, that's easier said than done. Wanting to be a part of the NCA and actually being there are entirely different things. Questions and doubts crept into my mind time and again. Would I be able to make it? How? Was I capable enough? But I've always tried to keep myself away from negative thoughts and stay in the present and enjoy it as a gift. Now I have realized that things automatically fall in place. You just need to believe in yourself, do your bit and leave the rest to the Almighty.

My first hurdle was getting into the ZCA. My chance came at the Under-16 Vijay Merchant Trophy (2008–09) where I scored three consecutive half-centuries in knockout rounds, playing for Delhi. Sadly, we lost to Punjab in the final. Luckily for me, my performance still won me a ticket to the ZCA North Zone camp, which was held that year at Palam in New Delhi. This was my first specialized camp organized by the BCCI (Board of Cricket Control of India). Thirty cricketers from North Zone (Delhi, Punjab, Haryana, Himachal Pradesh, and Jammu and Kashmir) were selected for the camp based on their performances in the U-16 inter-state tournament. Three years later, a few of us from North Zone would go on to be part of the India U-19 team. It was at this camp that we met for the first time and began to form those relationships that would be strengthened over time. I learned many new things at the ZCA camp. The coaching staff was brilliant. I still remember Usman Ghani sir, our head coach, Nandan Phadnis sir, batting coach, Vinod Raghavan sir, bowling coach, Nishant sir, trainer, and Suresh sir, physio. They worked on our basics and strengthened them, preparing us for the bigger challenges ahead. Our techniques were monitored; we were taught new drills; we were tested medically and for fitness; and we also discussed the history of the game. We got a basic idea and understanding of the game and realized the aspects we needed to work on to improve ourselves. At that point, we had no idea how things worked, but today, when I rewind, I can fit the boxes in the empty spaces and see the complete journey.

And then, to my great relief and excitement, I was selected for the North Zone team. By a stroke of fortune, that was the only time that the All India Under-16 Hanumant Singh Trophy was conducted. I scored 402 runs and was declared the Man of the Tournament. The highlight for me was when David

Whatmore, then the director of the NCA, presented me with a bat and a pair of shoes. That performance improved my standing and I was chosen to be vice-captain of the All India Under-16 team, which was to play the Colonel Hemu Adhikari Trophy in the same month. I played a couple of good innings against the university team in the tournament and thus began my transition from Under-16 to Under-19. Once back from NCA, I became a regular member of Delhi's U-19 team. I played for Delhi U-19 for the next three years and my performances won me a place in the Under-19 NCA camp for three consecutive years. I ended up spending about a month every year at NCA since I was sixteen.

The NCA is the Mecca of cricket in India. So when I got into the camp of the thirty probables for the Under-19 World Cup, I was overjoyed. It is true that I had been expecting this call as I had had a good debut Ranji season with Delhi, but one shouldn't count one's chickens before they are hatched. I was both very excited and very nervous. The camp was forty days long and I was looking forward to meeting new players. Some of the players there I knew because I'd played with them, others were names that I had heard because they were big scorers, and the rest I had never heard of at all.

All of us assembled in the front lobby of our hotel, standing and gossiping in different groups. I wasn't particularly shy but I didn't manage to mingle with everyone. I had played a season of Ranji one-dayers, so people knew me by name. I remember I was trying to show off in front of them as if I was the best player. Our bus came and we set off for the NCA in the rain. Once we got there, we scattered: playing table tennis, relaxing on sofas, chatting in groups, playing with phones. That day we had medical tests and 'screenings'. The physios examined posture and movement, and marked different points of our bodies for measurement. They asked about ailments and injuries. I didn't really understand at the time why we had to undergo all these tests and measurements—or why, later, we'd work only on one particular thing— but now that I have reached the end of that part of the journey, I can connect the dots and see the role that each thing played in building the path till now. It really brings home to me how everything happens for a reason.

We were divided into three groups of ten players each, and we would practise together and rotate between batting, bowling and fielding. And, of course, a player specializing in his department of the game would spend more time doing that. For instance, a batsman would spend more time batting at the nets or doing various batting drills. Similarly, the bowlers would bowl to the batsmen at the nets and would also do single-wicket bowling drill, where there is no batsman at the other end and the bowler would put a cone in the good length area and try to hit that mark. This is also called 'spot bowling'. Fielding drills were compulsory for all. With time, as the players were handpicked down to the final fifteen, things began to be more precise and the selection, performance based.

It was at our second or third net session that Sandeep Patil, the then director of NCA, came to observe our batting. It was one of those occasions where I just felt that I didn't bat well. But he came to me and said that after a long time he was being impressed by someone's batting. He told me that I had a very stylish way of batting and he could see a big cricketer in me. He said I would go far if I kept working hard and stayed grounded. He even added that he didn't say such things to every other cricketer; by then, some of his predictions over the past twenty years had already come true in the form of Sachin Tendulkar and a few others. I don't know what is it that they see in someone's batting that makes them so sure while the other players are also equally good. Maybe, experience holds the key. However, I hold his comments in deep reverence, and will try not to disappoint him or myself.

The NCA has played a very big role in my development as a player. Training there has made me very aware of myself and my batting. The best thing there is the video footage they take of you while playing, which you can watch later and scan for problems with the help of experts. I never liked videos of my batting because I always found I was making many mistakes. While watching the footage, we would get down to the very basics like stance, grip, backlift and so on. Obviously, everybody has their own style of batting and bowling—there is no unique way of doing it, and you can't teach everyone just one specific model. If it worked that way, the likes of Malinga and Muralitharan would not have come into existence at all. But at the NCA, they push you to try and get as close to copybook technique as possible.

This has often drawn criticism and scrutiny. But as a player, I don't think it is wrong of the coaches at the NCA to recommend that we make minor changes. Surely, it cannot harm you that you are getting closer to perfection. Still, even before I attended the camp, I had heard many players express discontent about the ways they teach at NCA, and coaches and fellow players told me not to listen to whatever was taught at the NCA and keep playing the way I had done so far. Some people say that the coach who has known you since your very first day is the one who knows you the best, and you should always listen to that coach over everyone else; the coaches at NCA had not seen me from the start of my career, so they couldn't say anything about my batting and that I should listen only to my old coaches. Well, I'm not entirely convinced by this. Neither extreme is good—whether you belong to the group that believes blindly in the copybook or blindly in having known the player from the very beginning.

I guess there are some players who are not ready to learn. There's no harm in unlearning a bit and trying out new things. One can always return to one's original style if one wants to. One should have at least that much faith in oneself. I went to the NCA with an open mind.

Diary Entry
19 July 2010

A new member joined the NCA today: Mike Young, Australia's fielding coach. He has come to spend a week with us and help us in the fielding department. He is a big man with a big heart. He shared his experiences with the Australian team and the IPL's Deccan Chargers (he's also their fielding coach). It was great to spend time with him. I have had two sessions with Mike, and I learned a lot from him. Mike has a very interesting method: he doesn't use a bat to make us do the drills; he just sits and watches us play and then tells us where we were going wrong. His main focus was on rhythm, not speed. He particularly told me to calm down and do the basics right and just follow the correct process—the outcome will definitely will be good.

After the sessions, he chatted with us for an hour, and shared a few key points. He paid attention to the throwing technique and gave us lots of tips. The straighter the path of the throwing arm, the higher the accuracy. We should always aim at the base of the stumps and move in the direction of the throw after the ball is released. While fielding, the ball should be rotated among the players as much as possible. This makes you more aware on the field. Whenever there is a chance to effect a run out, one should go for it. This is the secret of Australia's success. Mike's presence definitely made a lot of difference. For the first time in my life, I am thinking of my throwing, why I missed the stumps, etc. He has made us think about certain things that were missing from our minds so far. For instance, if I throw the ball to the right side of the stumps, I should position myself in such a way that the next time I throw, it should be aimed to the left of the previous throw. If I am able to do that it would mean I have improved; slowly, I will be able to hit the stumps more often. The alignment of the arm and the body should be towards the target and it is important to continue moving in the direction where you have thrown the ball.

I asked him how to deal with the negative feelings that always follow after dropping a catch or when the ball is not coming into your hands well and you tend to fumble it. He said that the best thing to do is to just calm down. A lack of confidence puts people on the back foot and they respond by getting overly defensive when what they really need to do is attack. Don't wait for the ball to come to you; sometimes you need to go to the ball. He said that fielding is about anticipation. Don't stand back. Sometimes you are nervous when in the field, and you try to avoid the ball, but the ball will find you. Step up and take it. Think as if every ball is coming to you and visualize yourself receiving the ball into your hands. Watch it till the last moment.

The art of batting: it's all in the technique

The best thing I got out of the NCA was an improvement in my batting. I have always thought that getting close to the copybook technique helps you to improve your batting because everything is connected. If you hold your bat in a certain way, it increases or decreases your chance of playing certain shots. It also gives an indication of the areas that may trouble you or of ways that increase your chances to get out. This really helped me. All the other batsmen used to watch their videos with the coaches and come out after five minutes. But I wouldn't come out of the room until I was totally satisfied. I used to go on until the point when I was absolutely clear in my mind about what was happening, how it could affect my way of batting, how I could improve it and what changes I should make to minimize the recurrence of the problem. I would then practise the solution for a few days under the proper supervision of coaches, and if it didn't work, we would try something else, and so on until I cracked it. In a month at the NCA, I would have tried ten to twelve methods to tweak my batting, and it helped. I became so much aware of my batting that I knew what I was doing. I understood why my body was behaving in a certain way. I had many faults. For example, I used to crouch sideways (sort of a C-shaped curve), so my weight was too much on the front foot even before playing the ball, so I was not able to take a big stride forward. This meant that my front foot stride was shorter than it should have been and, since my head was up and ahead, I used to chase the ball from far away without my feet getting close to the ball, and then I couldn't keep my balance. I used to 'walk'. One thing that irritated me was my front foot not being stable. I used to play the ball even before stabilizing my front foot on the ground. My front foot would be inclined while I played the ball and stabilized after that. It was as though I was taking out my front foot and meeting the ball before it actually landed properly.

Asking questions a must

If something didn't work, I always went back to the coaches, discussed it and then we would work out a new way. I was always after Nanawati sir (the then head of the NCA batting department) and company, who were really helpful. I used to ask many questions about my batting; I would discuss it in a group or have a chat with an international player. My friends used to tease me for this. They used to say that I was trying to impress the coaches, and buttering them up. I didn't like that. Sometimes I even got upset but it still didn't stop me from asking questions. It was not that I was asking questions just for the sake of asking them—I genuinely wanted to know. I wanted to learn as much as I could. That's the way I have always been. When I was in school, I used to ask my teachers questions until I was thoroughly sure I had a clear understanding of the concept. I find that many cricketers have a very narrow outlook. I wonder if it is because many of them don't come from educated families; sometimes they don't manage to finish school. I understood that my own background had given me some advantages, and I never doubted myself—I did whatever I felt was right irrespective of what others might think or say.

At some point, I realized that I couldn't be the same

way with everyone. I was from a different background from most of the people there, and I realized that as long as I kept myself away they would not accept me, so I began to try to understand them and be like them. By that time they had started thinking of me as a stuck-up guy. I wasn't considered a good guy and they were looking at me with suspicion. All this was because I was aloof. But the coaches and staff at the NCA really liked me—I had a healthy relationship with all of them. But the other players didn't. I knew that these boys were not interacting with them because they were nervous and unsure of themselves. They hesitated to speak in a gathering; perhaps they were afraid of what others would think, or that they would look foolish. Maybe they even believed that all this talking was nonsense. But I knew from the beginning that this was going to help me a lot—that it was going to take me where I wanted to go, right to the top— and I refused to let such things bother me.

But soon I realized that an aloof approach wouldn't take me far. After all, cricket is a team sport. So I started to mingle with everyone. Though I knew there were some who were talking about me behind my back, I tried to stay on good terms with everyone in the group. But still something happened that I will never forget. We went on a camping trip to Bhadra

Wildlife Sanctuary. Two or three boys had chalked out a plan to bully me. Paul [name changed] asked everyone to write on a piece of paper the name of the most disliked and hated person in the group. After everyone had written the name down, the slips were collected and Paul read the names aloud. Only he wasn't reading out the actual names written on the slips. He read out what he wanted to. So twenty out of the twenty-four had voted me as the most hated person in the group. It hurt me so much that I was instantly in tears. I wasn't angry but something inside me was hurting, thinking that I had never done anyone any wrong and had always tried to help everybody. Their behaviour was just shocking. I don't remember ever feeling like that in my whole life, before or after. This was beyond my control. I was hurt not because of those who were hostile towards me; I was hurt because of those who I had thought were good friends. I don't know how, but they did me in with the sweetest of smiles, all the time carrying daggers behind their backs.

What got me through this was the fact that somewhere inside me I knew why they did this. Their minds were prejudiced and closed to new things, to different experiences. The mind should always be clean; it should be able to grasp the necessary things, while automatically deleting the rest. It should always be open to new things, interesting suggestions and unusual ideas. If you don't try anything and remain the same old factory, then I am sorry, you can't sustain yourself for very long. You need to keep trying; that's the only way you have a chance of finding out whether something will click or whether something will suit you; that's what will help you in your game and your life.

I was lucky to have friends I could confide in: I poured my emotions out to my schoolmates, Utsav and Arjun, and told my uncle the whole story. All of them helped me calm down and regain my balance. Then an insight struck me: the right way to deal with the situation was to let it not affect me and I should mingle with them more and win them over. It was the better strategy because we were a team and we had to bond.

3

Donning the Skipper's Cap

One of the advantages of being captain is being able to ask for advice without necessarily having to take it.

—James T. Kirk

My first stint as a captain at state level was when I was in my second year playing for U-19 Delhi (DDCA) team, in 2010. I was to lead the team at the inter-state tournament for the Vinoo Mankad Trophy. I had some experience of captaincy—back in 2004, I had captained DPS in an inter-school tournament. I was in class IV then. We had won the tournament, and what was more, I was declared the Man of the Tournament. I can still remember Chetan Chauhan sir giving me both the winners' and Man of the

Tournament trophies at a specially organized ceremony in my school. Then I went on to lead Modern School and my club team. Now I was delighted to be given the opportunity to lead the Delhi U-19 team.

The general norm for these junior tournaments is to choose as captain the player who is an excellent cricketer and is also the most experienced. Since I was amongst the best players in the group at that time, I was almost a natural choice for captaincy. Another factor in my favour was that I had already played Ranji one-dayers for Delhi and performed well there. I had also performed well in the previous U-19 Cooch Behar Trophy, scoring 475 runs in seven matches. The other advantage I had was that I was a batsman. I have observed that a batsman is always given priority over a bowler when it comes to captaincy.

Captaincy was a great learning experience. I remember one incident when Delhi was playing a Cooch Behar Tournament match against Gujarat at St. Stephen's ground. It was the second day of the match and the umpires had signalled bad light because of fog and the match had stopped. In the meantime, I was speaking to Vinay Lamba sir (chairman of the U-19 selectors) and he was telling me about the importance of batting and cohesion within the team. As soon as he finished his lecture, a few teammates joined us. He wanted me to tell them what he had just told me. I proceeded to convey to them all he'd told me, in my own words. He stood there listening to me, and then commended the way I had interpreted and conveyed his thoughts, because, he said, communication is a vital part of leadership, and my ability to convey so clearly what he'd said was an indicator that I had the potential to be a good captain.

That episode made me appreciate that a captain's major role is to communicate effectively with his players. The better a captain communicates, the easier it becomes for his teammates to follow. Everything becomes simple and transparent. The team understands the goal and focuses on it. If there is even a slight communication gap between the captain and the players, it can cause a lot of chaos in the team. I knew at that instant that I should never allow any sort of communication gap in the team. All good leaders are good interpreters and good communicators. The right information at the right time always does the trick. Many historic battles were won because the right information was circulated in the battalion; the right signals, the right orders at the right time have made the difference between conquerors and losers. Human history is full of inspiring stories about how small armies won against the odds using communication as an effective tool. The great Indian rebellion of 1857 against the British Army was suppressed primarily because of the lack of communication among the rebel forces.

Good communication between a captain and his players is so important that it was slotted—following a brainstorming session at Nagarhole by a group of coaches—second on our list of the top three most important things that could help us win the World Cup. But captaining a side like Delhi is not that easy. There are many pressures working on you simultaneously. At times I was not given the players I wanted, and had to carry the burden of players I didn't really want. At first I was very angry, but then I realized that I had to get results with the limited resources available—that was the way to prove my mettle as captain. There would always be things that were not in my control; it made no sense to complain. I was going to have to get the best out of the players I was given. And so I set out to take the team to the top.

You see, it was very simple. If the team didn't win its matches, it would not get to play in the knockouts. And if the team didn't play in the knockouts, it just meant each of us would have fewer opportunities to display our talents and be recognized. And the less we were seen, the less likely it would be that we would be selected. I tried to make everyone realize this fact and become a bit selfish. I told them that our aim was not limited to playing this tournament—we had to excel and be selected for the zonal camp. So if we lost early, we would not be selected as our scores would be lower than those of the players whose teams reached the semi-finals and final. Also, the most number of players are selected from the winning team.

I had to use my players very judiciously, so my strategy was to use the weak bowlers when our team was in a strong position, and the moment I smelt danger, I would bring in my main bowlers. It's also very important to be good to everyone and maintain a healthy relationship with your mates and the support staff when you are captain. Any sort of misunderstanding, hatred or jealousy can make the team suffer. Ego clashes between captain and players and captain and the support staff can have really adverse impact on the team's performance and so sometimes, because you are captain, you have to be the first person who decides to set your ego aside. It was a tough lesson that I had to learn at a fairly young age. But it was worth it, because it really helped me to manage my players well during the World Cup.

Performance is the key

A leader does not actually lead; he is someone who guides people and they follow him faithfully. You don't need books to become a leader. Leaders are born. There is a saying: leaders don't read history, they create history. Well, I am not here to create history. Actually, I don't really believe in that sort of saying—but it is one of those things that have stuck in my head. I try to remain open to ideas and I like to keep them simple. I do read books on leadership. I don't mug it up but just read carefully. Some points that strike me stay with me, the others are flushed out. You don't have to remember everything; whatever works will enter your system if you read carefully and consciously, and then you apply things as and when situations demand. Your instinct, your inner voice does it for you. Everything you read and find good becomes part of your instinct. Once this is done, you just need to follow it and everything else falls into place automatically. It's not rocket science.

Performance is the key to leadership. Whether you are captain or not, you need to perform. And when you are captain, performing becomes even more important because everyone looks up to you. It is also really important to perform because it will draw the respect and support of your team, and unless and until you have that, you cannot lead it properly.

I have had good and bad phases of performance, and once that happened I understood how much it can affect your image in the team. First of all, good performance gives you loads of confidence, which comes to the fore when you lead. You take brave decisions. You act boldly. You feel powerful. The confidence helps you to take the right decisions. It's not that decisions are always right beforehand; often, it is your belief in yourself and in other players that makes them right. Confidence and self-belief are the most important traits that can help you cross any hurdle in life, not just in a cricket tournament.

However, if you don't perform, it becomes difficult to handle your mates. You lose that charisma. Somewhere deep inside you, you feel guilty and that guilt stands in the way of doing the right things. It can even show in your voice, but you won't know. You may have heard the adage that fortune favours the brave. But there is a very thin line between bravery and foolishness. Captaincy is something you can do with deliberate effort only up to a point; after that it's something that comes from within. If you try to be brave, you might end up taking some foolish decisions. So you can't force it. It has to be natural, and for that to happen you need to feel good about yourself. You should always feel full of life. How can you give others support if you yourself are not happy and full of confidence?

And honestly, if you can't think properly and ensure you're on top of your own game and in total control of yourself, how can you think about the team? I keep hearing people say that X is a team man, he plays for the team and Y is not a team man, he is selfish. People make up their minds based on what they get to see. They know whether you are a selfish player or a team player from the way you play. How you play is very transparent; it reveals everything. There are only two ways to play: playing protectively, where you play with a mindset that hampers the team's performance; and playing with your heart. There is a big difference between the two methods. You play with your heart when you are full of confidence and when you are not afraid of taking risks—a risk is not a risk for a confident man. But you play selfishly when you are not complete, when you lack something. So it's really important for both captain and players to keep performing in such a way that their instincts work for them.

Whenever I hear or think of or see something that seems important to me, I make a note of it. I call it my memo. One day, I was going through the memo on my phone and I discovered yet another very important point. I remembered that I had written this point last year, not in the context of captaincy but while focusing on my batting and overall personality. I was probably going through a lean patch and wasn't able to score well. I was a bit depressed, with constant thoughts of failure peeping in whenever I went in to bat. The tension and desperation were clearly visible on my face, and they affected my attitude towards other people too. As my confidence fell, I began to think and talk negatively, and lost my pride and enthusiasm. I asked everyone how to come out of it, thinking that someone could help. Of course, people did help me but I had also given them the chance to dominate me. I was falling down mentally and they were rising over me. At times my teammates would share light moments of laughter and pull my leg. That was OK. It doesn't take much time for me to overcome such things.

Sharing light moments is an important part of being a cricketer and being part of a team, but I feel there is a fine line between that and being mocked at, and you really shouldn't give people the chance to make fun of you. I am not saying that you should behave arrogantly or fight with someone who laughs at you; I mean that you should care for your public image, and prevent it from getting damaged. And it all depends on you—you are the only person who can make it happen. If you keep hearing negative things from people, it will destroy your confidence. So avoid negativity; that's the trick. Stay away from people who make negative comments, who criticize you or make fun of you. At no time should you allow people to take advantage of your failures. Ideally, failure itself shouldn't bother you. When you're doing badly, you should try to remain calm. Sooner or later, your performance will improve. But never show to your opponents and to your teammates that you are feeling low. Always keep smiling and never let people know what's actually going on inside you, however disheartened or disgusted you feel.

This was a very important lesson I learned, and one that I apply even when I am on the field: when the chips are down, no matter how important the match and its outcome, never let your anxiety show.

But as we all know, that is easier said than done. It's worth it though, because it has a profound effect on your teammates and opponents. When you're captain, it's important not to 'lose it' in crunch situations. A glum or tense face can ruin your chances as quickly as a relaxed, smiling face can erase the tension in the team, because everyone in the team looks up to you. If you yourself are down, how can you expect your mates to raise their spirits? And if you're always relaxed and cheerful, the opposition is at a loss because they can't tell what you're thinking, and can never take full advantage of the situation. If they see you panicking though, they will feel better and will have better control over the match.

There can't be a better example of a self-assured, nonchalant leader than our Captain Cool, Mahendra Singh Dhoni. His calmness and cool head have given him immense success. We are all aware of his cricketing prowess. What we don't understand is how much of it has to do with his mental skills. He always stays cool. It's not that he is not tense or under pressure at times; he just never lets it affect his attitude; it never shows on his face. This is a trait that can work wonders for you as a leader. A cool head can think better in hot situations.

4

Ranji Lessons

I've missed more than 9000 shots in my career. I've lost almost 300 games. 26 times, I've been trusted to take the game-winning shot and missed. I've failed over and over and over again in my life. And that is why I succeed.

—Michael Jordan

I vividly remember the day when I got the call telling me that I'd been selected to play one-day matches for Delhi in the Vijay Merchant Trophy. I was playing a match for Modern School and had got out after scoring 70. It had been an easy match and we were all hanging out in the dressing room and chatting. There were strong rumours that I might get selected to the senior state team, so I was pretty nervous—the selection meeting was in progress. I had never before been in such a state of nervousness. I was eagerly waiting for the news to come out. I was extra tense because I'd had mixed responses about my performance. Some people would say I was in for sure, but others would say I might have to wait another season. I had had a good Under-19 season that year, and Delhi's regular opener Aakash Chopra had shifted to Rajasthan, creating a vacancy in Delhi's top order. My school coach asked whether the meeting was over, and soon he himself announced that I'd been included in the senior side!

I was ecstatic. My excitement surpassed all limits. All my teammates congratulated me. I got many calls from the media that day. I was so excited that I was all over the place. I was sixteen years old and studying in class XI. I was so happy because I had set myself the goal of playing Ranji before I turned seventeen, and I had so done it! (I had mentioned this in my diary a year ago. Read the excerpts on page 49.) But the feeling of excitement can only last so long and eventually the thrill died down. True excitement lies in continuing to do the work that you love.

I joined the camp the very next day. I was slightly nervous as I would be facing the likes of Virat Kohli, Shikhar Dhawan, Ishant Sharma, Ashish Nehra and Mithun Manhas. I already knew Rajat Bhatia from school. It was a great feeling to practise in the nets with the players I had grown up watching. At first, I was just watching them and feeling happy just to be a part of the group. They were all very kind to me. I bonded with Virat and Shikhar very well. In fact, after watching me bat in the nets, Virat came to me and discussed a few things. He was really encouraging and told me how to deal with the pressure and people's expectations. Virat had also faced the same problems that I had, and he gave me excellent advice on how to deal with politics and the messy interactions that happen in those situations. He told me to stay close to people who make me feel positive.

Virat was not the only person to give me advice—those were the days when advice just poured in from all sides. Most of my well-wishers told me to stay grounded. I was told that many talented players had not made it big because they remained satisfied merely with Ranji. I was advised to stay in the company of good players from whom I could learn and derive confidence and good vibes. It really gave me a boost. I started growing in those surroundings and learned a lot about dressing room activities. Virat and Shikhar are like thermostats. They change the atmosphere of the dressing room. They bring unmatchable life to the field and the dressing room. I imbibed lots of confidence just by being around them.

And then there was the real cricket. I remember my debut against Jammu and Kashmir. I was very nervous as I faced my first ball—but that is normal; it happens to everyone. But I got off to a flier, dispatching the first two balls for a boundary, which really relieved the pressure. After that, however, the bowlers stuck to one line and I was unable to find the gaps, which is when I learned the importance of singles. I scored only 25 runs, including a six—and then got out while trying to go for another one when there was no need. I didn't know it at the time, but I would get out in a similar fashion in a few more matches and feel very disappointed about it.

In the second match against arch-rivals Punjab, I scored a brisk 74 off 49 balls. It was the best knock I had played till then. Shikhar and I had a 150-run opening partnership in just 18 overs before I got out once again playing a lofted shot. I was disappointed but happy to score my first half-century in List A matches. It was a great feeling to play with such big players. It felt great to bump fists with Shikhar and Virat as the match went on. It made me feel on top of the world, and my confidence soared tremendously.

Unfortunately, I was dropped after the third match— I had played that same uppish shot for the third consecutive time, and was out again. I did make many mistakes in my first season but I certainly learned a lot. Over the years, with practice and experience, I have seen the difference in my batting. Today, I can easily see the difference between my present state of mind and what it was two years back. There has been a significant change in my approach. Success depends on how you grow and understand your game. But a word of caution: Too much maturity is also not good. Bob Dylan says that as you mature and grow older, things actually get more difficult sometimes, because maturity brings with it a tendency to analyse, which when it goes too far, can hinder your progress. You then begin to try to control your creative impulses. Many sportsmen succeed not because of their experience but because of their inexperience. Experience brings wisdom to some but to others, it makes them overanalyse. Sometimes you simply learn new impediments to creative self-expression, and then you have to unlearn them. For instance, a young poet writes freely. But once he learns about life and has a lot of experience under his belt, say, when he crosses the age of fifty, his creativity can vanish. He might start thinking too much and see life as a very complicated thing, beyond his ability to articulate. Which makes it a good idea to hold on to some immaturity—your inner child, if you may.

Creativity is something that comes from inside yourself. Yes, it can be triggered by something external, but at the end of the day, it lies within you. It's something that has to be cultivated, nurtured and respected. Constant intellectual intervention can block your creativity. You have to programme your brain to not think too much. Although I strongly believe that nothing should be left to chance, there are always a few things that just happen for you without much thought. If you look at this sort of magic stuff too carefully and try to take it apart and figure out how it works, it might not happen again. If you bring a highly trained and deeply intellectual gaze to bear upon the magic, it might fall apart. This is something you need the wisdom to recognize. But I don't mean to say don't bring in analysis at all. Nothing happens automatically. You have to work hard and practise deliberately and it has to be well designed and goal oriented. Performance is always conscious and under our control, not automatic. Great performers achieve the ability of avoiding the automated routes. Deliberate practice over the years brings you to a state when you start performing without any thought, it's automatic and that's when you are in your so-called 'zone', which is not easy to achieve. The balance to be struck is while you need some planning, at the end of the day you have to listen to your instincts.

5-8-2009

Winning or loosing doesn't matter. Without the loosers, there are no winners. But we should know how to win graciously and how to loose with dignity.

01 SATURDAY

17-8-2009

I have to make it to the Ranji Trophy squad before I turn 17.

- Achieved

This diary resolve turned out exactly the way
Unmukt wanted it to.

Diary Entry
Ranji Season 2010–11

This Ranji Trophy season has been very special for me. Though we couldn't qualify for the knockouts, the five matches I have played have really taught me a lot about this game. I was really fresh at the start of the season and full of confidence after being the highest scorer in the Under-19 one-day matches. I got a call for the Delhi Ranji squad for the third match against Gujarat that we were to play at Feroz Shah Kotla. I really batted well but couldn't capitalize on a good start. In my first two matches I fell a victim to negative bowling, or perhaps I was not mature enough to resist the temptation to hit out at the balls outside the off stump, while the opposition was mature enough to persist with the same line of attack. As I played more matches, however, I was gradually able to curb myself. It was after I scored two consecutive half-centuries that I felt a sense of belonging. It's important to have this feeling of belonging. These couple of quick but short innings bolstered my confidence. It was only due to my increasingly insatiable hunger for a big score that I was able to play a gritty knock of 151 against Railways on the grassy wicket of Roshanara grounds. It was one of the best knocks that I have ever played, but even more importantly, I scored when my team needed it the most. It feels good to contribute to the team's cause.

It's funny how much easier it is to learn by messing up. I mean until you screw up, you don't really understand how it works; until you make mistakes, you don't learn—well, for me anyway. I'm sure there are people who can learn before they've made any mistakes, but those people are geniuses! The rest of us learn better after a slight setback. Cricket especially is a kind of sport that makes you learn from your mistakes. As far as those 151 runs go, I couldn't have scored those runs if I hadn't got out chasing wide balls in the earlier matches. So, I subconsciously learned not to fall into the trap of the opposition by chasing wide balls. And now when I see the video of that match, I'm surprised to see myself leaving so many balls. I was in full control of myself. Everything went very slow that day—maybe it had to do with my regular meditation sessions. Then again, experts talk about 'being in the zone'; perhaps I was in my zone that day.

Unfortunately, we lost the game. I couldn't take my team through in the second innings. This meant that our next match, against Mumbai, was a do-or-die one for us. We desperately needed a win. But we were unable to take the first innings lead. I got out to Ajit Agarkar in that innings. I couldn't focus. I was trying to fiddle with every ball; mentally, I was distracted. In the second innings there was nothing much left in the match but still I got out to such a horrendous shot that I still regret it. I could have easily collected more runs. I cannot blame anyone but myself for playing like that in that match. But there was an important lesson to be learned from there too. Before this match, one of my school coaches had exaggerated the situation a bit. He had told me that if I hit a century, I might be considered for the Indian team, as scoring against Mumbai always counts. It weighed too much on my mind; I was too excited to be able to play normal cricket. I started expecting even more from myself.

This went against me and put unnecessary pressure on my game. I couldn't enjoy myself at the crease. I was constantly reminding myself to score a ton; I was not living in the present. Until then I had been playing carefree, just enjoying my game, because I wasn't too worried about the outcome. But things were different in this match. That's where I learned how important it is to live in the present and not let the pressure of the future and your or other people's expectations bother you.

The other thing I learned this season is to believe in myself. I have often been told to curb my shots. I have been told not to play in the area I preferred (square of the wicket). But I am happy to say that I was reluctant to do as I was told. Those are the areas that fetch me runs; if I don't play those shots, I will never score! But at the same time, it's equally important to know when to avoid playing certain shots, even if they are your strengths; it's important to play according to pitch conditions and the match situation. These have to be kept in mind for better results. Though I feel playing in the 'V' (mid-off to mid-on region) is always a safer option, especially when the ball is new and playing tricks. Eventually, after settling down, you can open up and play more freely.

I also realized that I had to be very careful about taking advice from others. I found everybody around me playing coach but I had to be shrewd about selecting the tips that would work for me. There's a big difference between playing to win and playing to not lose. It's important to keep the 'play to win' approach and avoid the 'play to not lose' one. You have also got to keep away from people with a negative attitude. At the end of the day, you should know what you are doing and the reason behind it. Never do things without understanding and choosing the purpose behind them.

In a country like India, advice is free and in a game like cricket, anyone from a CEO of an MNC to a roadside paanwalla can teach you how to play. It's sometimes funny to hear people gossiping in groups on the performance of a player, his limitations and weaknesses; it would seem as if they could do a better job than him. At such times, I feel like going up to them and telling, 'Excuse me, why don't you yourself go and play?' I mean it's so easy to blame and point out a person's mistakes. But do we ever appreciate the hard work that goes behind the scene? NO. We Indians are tough taskmasters. No good results and they'll tell that you've got a whole bunch of wrong habits creeping into your system: 'oh, my god, success has gone to his head'; 'of late, he's been partying too much'; 'nah, he's not serious any more, he's sold out to fame and glamour'.

But as soon you start performing, the reactions change swiftly and suddenly you become a good boy: 'oh, I've heard he's working really hard'; 'he's not partied for the last five months'; 'he has improved so much'. Blah-blah . . . Sick! I mean, take a break, guys. Stop interfering and making life difficult for us.

We've been brought up in an environment that says: you shouldn't, you can't, you are not supposed to. There's no liberty, no freedom. If you set yourself free, then you're one spoilt and arrogant brat. People don't like those who set out on their own journeys, who stay happy and positive. They want such people to struggle; they want them to listen to their inanities. I'm not pointing fingers at anyone in particular, but that's how our system works. You are supposed to go through the grind and toe the line, then only you're accepted. But there too, you are unsure about what goes on behind your back.

Then one fine day, you become a star but still you are not let free. Everyone wants to take credit: 'look, I made him'; 'that advice I gave him that day, see, he has matured so much since then, his outlook has changed, his cricketing abilities have touched the skies'; 'he's my product'. Oh please, will you please give me a break?

But soon, you start to understand the entire psychology and chain of events. You stop caring about what people say. Then, it gets worse: 'Look at him, he was nothing when he came to me and see now he's ignoring me. These stars have their heads in the stars, they are selfish.' The whole point I am trying to make is that life is never easy for a cricketer, especially one who has played for the country and is a star. He has to learn to deal with stardom and all its brickbats and bouquets.

Of course, I do understand the love and fervour of Indians when it comes to cricket. All of us love this game and being associated with it in any manner is the least we could all do. Our heart beats for this game. If cricket had meant nothing to us, then who would have bothered about cricketers. Cricket would have been just another game. Heroes are not born, they are made. By the fans. They pray for their heroes' success from the bottom of their heart. When it comes to watching their heroes play, they give up on everything else: appointments, schedules, duties . . . So, we as cricketers have to understand that if we have been made real-life heroes, then we are accountable to those who have made us so. They love us so much that they have every right to caution us, advise us, and occasionally, meddle into our personal lives. As our well-wishers, even our guardians, they expect us to remain true and remember the roots from where it all started.

5

A Shot in the Arm

If you are not going all the way, why go at all?

—Lou Holtz

By the time our first U-19 tournament started, our team had gelled nicely. We were playing in a four-nation series comprising India, Sri Lanka, West Indies and Australia. It was to be held at Vizag. Our camp was an excited lot. During the pre-series preparation, we had had a great time at the NCA. It was fun to practise and train there. Here I need to mention each of our coaching staff: B. Arun (head coach), R. Sridhar (fielding coach), Sudharshan V.P. aka Chetta (trainer), Srinivasan (physiotherapist) and Sanju Singh (video analyst). It was the best team I have ever worked with so far. I had never met such nice and understanding people who were always full of life. They made us feel like their friends. We used to laugh together, sweat it out together and then eat together at night.

As the tournament neared, there were talks about what the West Indian and Australian teams would be like. 'Is Pat Cummins also coming? He bowls at a speed of 150 km per hour.' 'You know there is a player called Braithwhite in the West Indies side who has already played Test cricket for his country.'

But we were never afraid.

We landed in Vizag and stayed in a five-star hotel next to the beach. Being the captain, I had a single room! It was amazing! It was plush and, as soon as I drew my curtains, I saw huge waves crashing on the shore. I just loved the view.

There was a lot of buzz in the hotel. During such tournaments generally, all teams stay in the same hotel on different floors so that players from different countries can meet and interact. On the eve of the inaugural match, the managers assemble for an official meeting with the umpires and match officials. The various rules and codes of conduct are discussed. I find this quite boring, and Arun sir and I have once attended such a meeting in casuals, while everyone else was in proper formals. I later realized that this was not a good thing and we too should have followed the rules.

A world record chase and a high-tension final

Our first match was against Australia. We wrapped them up for 162 runs. What happened next was phenomenal. A record partnership between Manan Vohra and me chased the target down in just 12 overs with a few big hits and the Aussies didn't know what hit them. It was a day when every ball just came on to my bat. Manan was on song at the other end. He was carrying the confidence from his fiery hundred in a practice match, and I was finding form at just the right time. To be completely honest, their spin attack was very poor and we cashed in on that. I scored 72 runs in just 40 balls with 11 boundaries and three sixes, while Manan scored 79 in 35 balls. There was a sort of competition between us to score faster. Later on, we were told that it was the fastest-ever chase in a one-day U-19 match!

The next match against Sri Lanka was a cliffhanger. Rush Kalaria was the hero of the match and we found a new bowling all-rounder in him. His batting skills at the lower order have got us out of crises several times. In this particular match, Sri Lanka batted first and scored 184 runs. It wasn't a massive target but you cannot take anything for granted in this game of cricket. It is known for its unpredictability; you don't win or lose a match until the last run is scored or the last wicket taken, or till the overs run out. Manan departed early in the innings. I was going hammer and tongs but couldn't keep at it for long. I got out at 28. Vihari held up one end and scored a much-needed 51 before falling into the Lankans' trap. Others got out in single-digit scores. All of us were sulking in the dressing room and none of us held any hope of winning until Rush came out as an angel to make his magic. He played 81 balls to notch up an unbeaten, match-winning knock of 47. Kamal Passi also contributed by holding on at the other end and helping Rush finish the task. It was an incredible win and Sri Lanka lost their only chance of beating us. We never allowed them to come so close again.

We easily pulled off a victory against West Indies in our third league match. I scored a half-century. My first U-19 ODI century came against Sri Lanka in the fifth league match. I scored an unbeaten 122 while chasing the target of 200 runs. We topped the league table with an unbeaten record, while Sri Lanka came in second. So it was to be an India–Sri Lanka final.

There was a lot of excitement in the dressing room

before the final. Being the unbeaten and form team of the tournament, the momentum was in our favour. We followed our routine and I could see the excitement and eagerness on each of our faces for the showdown against Sri Lanka. This was our first Under-19 tournament and we were on a winning spree. As the captain, I wanted my team to just relax. So just before the final, I took the team to the naval base in Vizag. My uncle has some friends in the Indian Navy and he had fixed up the trip to the base. Luckily, at that time INS *Shakti* had been commissioned to the navy and we were fortunate enough to explore that grand ship. We learned all sorts of things about the ship. It has a self-defence capability and is equipped with an indigenous 'anti-missile defence chaff system'. On-board systems include fully automatic engine controls, power-management and battle-damage control systems. According to the navy, the ship was designed to operate as a command platform.

The captain of the ship was kind enough to take us all over the ship, explaining the significance of each thing. It was awesome and an altogether new experience for us. We had a great time there and many of us felt more than ever that we were lucky in choosing cricket as a career. Who has got the time and stamina to study and get through engineering exams to join the navy and learn to operate a ship. It would not have been easy. We also went inside a submarine, only to discover that there was hardly any space in it, and all we could do was to bang our heads against all sides. In a submarine, you have to always bend to move from one compartment to another. Life inside it isn't easy; it's actually quite suffocating. Nonetheless, it was a good experience.

We came back from our break and prepared for the final. We were all charged up, especially after the grand party before the final. It's quite strange but we were always a confident lot, partying and celebrating even before the final as if we knew we were going to win. Ramesh Rao (Anna) was the host. He is a big-hearted man. He booked a beachside restaurant for us and we all had a great time there, dancing crazily to the non-stop drumming. But no one was allowed to have alcohol. Our trainer had told us not to even have soft drinks during the tournament and we all followed his instruction religiously. That was the hallmark of this team. In all the tournaments till the World Cup, everyone abided by the rules. We reminded each other of them. I have never seen such cohesiveness in a team; we were always there for each other. That was going to be the biggest factor in our becoming world champions.

On the day of the final, we tried to replicate the things that we had done in earlier matches. While my luck with the toss was abysmal, I got lucky in other areas: whenever it mattered the most, the team pulled together, like in the quadrangular final and the World Cup final. My teammates used to tease me about my luck or lack of it with the toss. They would say that I should practise my tossing and calling skills, or else should get someone else to go for the toss on my behalf. And the times I did win the toss, my mates would look at me with utter surprise and amusement.

In the final I lost the toss as usual—my tally of lost tosses rising to five out of seven in the tournament. We were asked to bat first. The Vizag wicket, as we had seen all through the tournament, didn't support batting, especially in the first innings. The early moisture and the loose nature of the track made it difficult to score easily. The wicket would get better over the day. We struggled as our batting collapsed. I was unfortunately run out on 14, while Manan scored just 2. Then Akshadeep came to our rescue and scored a crucial 55. We managed to set a target of 168, our lowest score in the whole tournament.

But after winning six matches on the trot, we were in no mood to mess up the final encounter. Moreover, we had beaten Sri Lanka twice in the league stage.

Right from the first ball, we were on top of them. The intensity was really high. The attitude was right and our momentum was at its peak. Sandy (Sandeep Sharma) gave the Sri Lankans a tough time and a few early wickets brought us right back into the match. But the target was small, so I knew it was just a matter of one good partnership and we would be struggling—which is exactly what happened. In these situations what matters most is self-belief. Despite that partnership, I don't think anyone in my team had any negative thought of losing, which is what helped us break the partnership.

At times like these, under difficult conditions and in high-pressure situations, instinct comes into play. What ends up working is intuition, or as Sridhar sir likes to call it, *educated guesswork*. I was getting messages from outside to do certain things. But I tried to follow my inner voice. At a crucial time, the penultimate over, I asked Rush Kalaria to bowl, while some thought Sandy would be the better option. But that particular over by Rush actually was the turning point. He took an important wicket and kept us alive in the match. Sandy bowled the last over—and trust me, it was a tough time to bowl. But Sandy handled the pressure really well, thanks to his vast experience. Sri Lanka needed just six runs and had two wickets left. But Sandy's expertise in bowling yorkers at the death with baffling consistency came into effect. The Vizag crowd was cheering for us and making a lot of noise. Sandy bowled the third ball of the last over and I found the ball coming to me. The next moment I had taken the catch. Sri Lanka was nine down. The crowd got noisier. We were all on tenterhooks as Sandy ran in hard. He bowled the fifth ball, a yorker, which crashed through the stumps and we were all over the park, shouting and cheering.

That final wicket was one of the best moments for our team. We jumped onto Sandy, shouted and cried our hearts out. Wow! What a moment that was! The media was all over the ground, capturing all our celebrations. We shouted and danced to our favourite numbers, 'Danza kudoro' and 'Bhag DK Bose'. Sandy was the hero! The celebration that followed is best told the way I did in my diary.

Diary Entry
9 October 2011

Victorious, we have come back to the hotel. Even the hotel staff greeted and congratulated us. A cake was arranged very quickly. Looking at the cake, I knew it was going to be splashed more on our faces than eaten. In a few moments I was having a cake bath. The cake was everywhere—it went into my ears and nose! YUCK!!!

As soon as we entered our rooms, we changed into our party clothes and it was time to enjoy ourselves. We had booked a banquet hall in the hotel and some special arrangements had been made. I opened the first champagne bottle of my life there and messed up the whole floor. My role was limited to just opening it, and my teammates were not going to leave me dry. We danced the whole night. Our star performers on the dance floor, Harmeet Singh and Passi set the tone. Harmeet has impressed me with his dance more than anything else. The way he moves his feet while dancing is so amazing that I have often teased him by saying that I wished he could replicate it while fielding. Passi on the other hand is the 'desi boy'. He can dance for hours and is loved by everyone for his desi andaaz and the way he speaks. I bet there cannot be another Passi in the world. He is a mad boy, very jovial. You need to have such guys in your team, guys who can lighten the atmosphere around. We became good companions later on.

Anyway, our journey is over and it is time for some domestic matches. For me it's time for my second Ranji season.

Quadrangular Series in Australia: March–April 2012

After the end of the Ranji season, it was again time to fly back to our second home, the NCA in Bengaluru. I hadn't had a good season. I failed to convert good starts into big scores. I was quite upset with myself and it was difficult to get out of that troubled mindset. It's always good to take some time off and clear your mind of such negative thoughts. I mean, you develop a kind of membrane/wall around yourself when you play with a single set of players and are not performing. It's difficult to play under adverse conditions, conditions that can arise sometimes from a negative environment and a lack of coordination and understanding. I faced a similar problem. Mindset is such an important aspect that it can change everything drastically. It all depends on who you talk to and what kind of atmosphere you live in. For me, whenever I am depressed and low on confidence, I try to be in a positive environment. Being with my U-19 mates was a big positive for me.

We played a few practice matches and I scored heavily in all of them. All of a sudden my confidence was back. Our next task was winning the second quadrangular series in Australia. It was our first tour abroad as a team. It was my second tour of Australia, and my first as captain.

It was a long flight via Singapore. We had lots of fun on the flight itself. I was sitting with Manan. He is my best buddy and I love spending time with him. He has a very sweet and friendly nature; he is also a serious cricketer. He makes me laugh a lot.

We landed in Brisbane at around 10 at night. It was a Sunday night, so unfortunately, everything was closed. We just had one night in Brisbane. The next day we were to board another flight to Townsville, two hours from Brisbane. We didn't expect Townsville to be a happening place since we knew it was a scarcely populated town. So we wanted to go around and explore the city of Brisbane. But the problem was that most of the players wanted to stay in the hotel and sleep. Only Harmeet, Passi and I had a tendency to be nocturnal. We wandered around the streets trying to find a good restaurant. But hardly anything was open except a few strip clubs where we could not have ventured, not just because the minimum age for entry was twenty-one but also because we did not want to start the tour in such a manner. Our Indian value system stopped us too. We came back, sat in Harry's room and tried to enjoy ourselves there, eating nachos with salsa and Maggi. While gossiping we didn't realize we had finished three packets of nachos. I never was a nachos guy but Harry's company got me addicted to them.

The next morning we were off to Townsville. I was so tired and short of sleep that I fell asleep immediately and was woken up when we landed. Townsville appeared a beautiful town. Later on, I was to develop a special relationship with this city and the Indian families living there.

We checked into our hotel. The location was perfect. The sun came right into my room and lit it completely. Just outside the balcony was the swimming pool and further down a small stream that connected to the huge Cleveland Bay. From my room you could see Flinders Street, Townsville's main attraction. It had all the night clubs, food joints and museums. Townsville is also on the Great Barrier Reef. I have no words to express the beauty of the place. Famished and sleepy, we quickly prepared on the microwave the two-minute meals that we had carried with us from India, filled ourselves and slept. Manan was sharing the room with me. We had to report in the evening at five for a light gym session. The dumb fellow didn't wake up to his alarm and both of us kept sleeping. When I got up, it was already 6 p.m. I did not know what to do. The team had already left and the two of us had been left behind. I kept my cool but Manan got really nervous and anxious. I knew Arun sir, our coach, was a cool person and he would not make a big deal of it, but Manan screwed my mind. Finally, as I expected, nothing happened. Arun sir had no problem. 'It happens after such a long flight. You were jet-lagged!' he said, and I smiled at Manan.

The next day we went for a practice session and saw the main stadium. It was quite picturesque. Our team was the last one to get access to the practice area as the wickets had already been occupied by the other three teams. It was a low track and so we didn't get a feel of the bouncy Australian tracks. We did some fielding and then packed up.

Fast and fiery: Welcome to Australia!

Our first match was against New Zealand the next day at Endeavour Park. New Zealand won the toss and chose to field. Manan and I opened the innings. Manan faced the first ball. It was a short-pitched delivery that kissed his nose and went to the keeper. Damn quick! From the non-striker's end, I glared at him and he sneaked a look at me. We looked at each other in amusement. It was as if we were saying: 'Good morning, buddy! Welcome to Australia!' The first 10 balls I faced, I either let them pass at chest height or, if I was able to put my bat to one, it hit just below the handle of the bat. It seemed as if there were springs on the pitch which made the ball hitting the deck come higher and faster. I was thinking that the same balls that I was leaving at chest height would have been dispatched for fours between point and cover boundary on numerous occasions on Indian wickets. But here these balls would go towards gully or slip.

The conditions were showing us up. It is never easy to play balls coming at you faster than 130 kph in such conditions, especially when you have never practised playing such quick bowling. Already, three of our batsmen were back in the pavilion. Then it was my turn. The first ball that I middled went straight to the fielder at cover, who took an excellent catch. I had played 21 balls and scored a meagre two runs. We were struggling. Wickets kept falling regularly. There was an Indian guy, Ish Sodhi, in the Kiwi side—he later became a good friend—who scalped three of the crucial wickets. Luckily, Akshdeep Nath and Baba Aparajith managed to spend some time at the middle and got the total to 123. Our batting had collapsed miserably. But then, as a batting unit, we had had many such shocks. Our bowlers had come to our rescue on such occasions, and so we were now banking on them. We bowled well and stretched the match till the 90th over, but ultimately we lost by six wickets. A few dropped catches, too, had not helped.

We had lost our first match of the tournament. Obviously not the perfect beginning to such an important tour. We had to turn the tables fast. The batsmen wanted to play as many balls as possible on Australian soil and the spinners wanted to work on their flight and pace. Readjustment was required.

Our next match was against Australia at the main stadium. It's a beautiful ground and I have fond memories of the stadium, owing to the fact that this was the place where history was made. Once again, I lost the toss and we were put in to bat. I was fast becoming the main culprit in my team's struggle—I mean, in those conditions the toss is of vital importance as the pitch becomes better for batting as the match progresses.

We needed depth in our batting. So we made some minor changes to our batting order. Manan and Akhil Herwadkar were to open the innings, while I was to come in at no. 3. Aparajith was also brought up the order because of his solid batting technique. We were sure the Australians wouldn't be able to break through his defence. Though I was initially unhappy about batting at no. 3, I accepted the slot once I realized it was for the good of the team. My coach didn't want me to get out early. He had the confidence in me that I could bat for a long time once I settled down. And the strategy somehow worked. I went in to bat in the ninth over and carried on from there. We were going great until I played a sweep shot to Ashton Agar (left-arm spinner) and was trapped in front of the wicket. I had made 45. We managed to get 260. Not bad.

Our bowling was our main weapon and we had never let any team score over 200 against us. But today turned out to be a different day. Kurtis Patterson and his partner hammered us. The wicket had become flat and nothing was really happening for the bowlers. We were playing with an extra spinner, which to many might seem a strange option in Australian conditions, but our reading of the pitch was that it was meant for two medium-pacers and three spinners. Our spinners had done a great job in the past; we also knew that non-subcontinental teams didn't read spin well, especially the Aussies as they were accustomed to fast pitches and fast bowlers. But it didn't work this time. As a captain I took it upon myself and bowled a few overs. I gave away just 24 runs in the five overs that I bowled and turned out to be the most economical of the bowlers. Patterson scored a brilliant 99 before he fell into a well-set trap. Kuldeep was bowling. He is a chinaman bowler (left-arm legspinner) and I was standing at long off for Patterson (left-hand bat). He was hitting the bowlers all over the park. When he reached 99, I stopped Kuldeep and came to mid-off to stop the single. Kuldeep hesitated on taking that field but I told him to bowl. As expected, Patterson came out of the crease and tried to clear me and missed the ball. He was brilliantly stumped. It was a smart tactic. It's really very important to listen to your instincts. As a captain I had felt the need to change the field for that particular ball. Instincts work a lot in cricket. The energy in the field was superb. Everyone tried to contribute but sadly the result wasn't in our favour. We lost the match in the final over.

I was surprised at the performance of the Australian team. We had bashed the same team back in India, but now they had a different body language. Down two matches, we were very upset but we knew a win wasn't far away. We had fared much better than in our previous match. We didn't crib about our losses. We had confidence in ourselves and were still hopeful of winning the tournament. At times, Arun sir used to get worried but it lasted only for a brief period. Sri sir would pull him up, saying, 'Don't underestimate my boys.' That was the best thing. The coach and support staff never put us under any sort of pressure. They were like our parents, protecting us and encouraging us to do better.

At night, by turns we would be called for dinner at Arun sir's room. Every one of us waited for our chance. Not many would know that Arun sir and Sri sir are superb cooks. Yummy! My mouth is watering even as I write these lines, remembering the taste of food we had at his room. While the players would go to Woolworths (a grocery shop) and buy ready-made meals, they would buy vegetables, raw chicken, prawns and fish. Oh man! What prawns! And the chicken he cooked! You would never be able to stop eating. I have no words for that kind of tasty stuff. And Sri sir used to make various kinds of salads that were equally delicious.

Our last league match was against England at Endeavour Park, and again I lost the toss. Again we batted first. But this time we had a good opening partnership. After Akhil got out in the 13th over I joined Manan, who was batting well. He scored 50 and then played a rash shot to get out. I was batting well too. Whenever I batted in my Under-19 matches, I have always felt as if I was the boss, the best in the world. This feeling came from within and my confidence was at its highest possible level. But when I was well set on 28, Vijay Zol ran me out. I was really furious. It was an absurd call from him, almost unbelievable. Frustrated, I walked back to the dressing room. Vijay is a good player but his reputation as a runner isn't. He needs to work on it. He, however, played well and scored 60, taking our score to 268. It was a defendable total.

England started well. They started demolishing our bowling attack. Daniel Bell-Drummond scored a century. He plays just like Gayle, though he is a right-hand bat. He is damn strong square of the wicket. He was hitting the ball so hard that even though we were standing on the circle, we were as careful as if we were fielding at short leg or silly point. Anything short would be dispatched to the midwicket boundary and anything outside off would pierce the field and go past the boundary like a rocket. He was a real threat. Finally, we got him but he had given England a solid start upon which the rest of their batsmen capitalized. The other batsman who impressed me a lot was Ben Foakes. He batted really well. All my bowlers were exposed, so I took the ball in my own hands. I was bowling well, giving three to four runs per over. I bowled the 48th over and gave away five runs. The match got intense. Mohsin bowled the 49th over, and he gave away 12 runs. Now England required 10 off the last over. I was in a conundrum. Who should be given the last over? I didn't want any of the spinners to bowl. Sandy was not playing in the match; otherwise, he would have been the obvious choice. Mohsin had bowled the previous over. So the two options were either me or Passi. I was very confident about myself. So after much deliberation, I decided to bowl but it backfired. The match was over by the fourth ball of the last over. I was hit for a four and a six. I was crestfallen. And so was the team. My heart sank. Losing the third match on the trot was heartbreaking. Arun sir was livid and for the first time, I feared of going anywhere near him.

Everyone was disappointed, though my teammates backed me as it was our collective decision to let me bowl the last over. But I heard some negative and hostile remarks from a mate which caused some bad blood between us. Later on, everything was fixed up with the due interference of Arun sir and Sri sir. I was feeling guilty. Time and again, I thought that I should have called Passi to bowl the last over. Later in the evening, Arun sir, Sri sir and we sat down to discuss the match. My last over had spoilt the match for us but even now when I think about it, I know that the situation was such that I had no choice. I couldn't have given Aparajith the ball as he flights it too much and could be easily hit at that time. Passi could have bowled but he didn't show any confidence that he could do it. I mean at that point I would have given the ball to anyone who had come up to me saying, 'Skipper, give me the ball. I will bowl the last over.' I didn't get any such response from anyone. Maybe that's why I decided to bowl myself. It's a different issue that I could not save the match. I think that at that juncture confidence is the lone thing that can help you succeed. Always support and back the person who shows confidence. The one thing I learned from the episode is that the crucial overs should always be given to the main strike bowlers, and not to part-timers (except in a few situations). It was a difficult night for me but things slowly settled down. Every new morning brings with it new hopes. The past goes by teaching you a few lessons, while the future awaits you as ever.

The rising and the cup

India was at the bottom of the points table. But the format of the tournament was such that all the four teams would qualify for the semis, so the league matches didn't matter much. (It was a friendly pre-World Cup practice tournament.) And though we were at the bottom of the table, most of the teams feared us. Even some of the Aussie officials came to me to predict that we were going to win the title. The atmosphere in our dressing room was still the same—vibrant and energetic. Self-belief was high. We knew that losing the first three matches didn't make a difference. We were going to rise up to the occasion when it mattered the most. It's always important to stand up when it counts. As we would always say, 'Our best quality so far has been to peak at the right time.' And we have really excelled at exhibiting this trait over and over again, personally or collectively.

We would sometimes make fun of the other teams' predicament, doing well in the league matches and losing to us in the knockouts. We were charged up for the semis. In the meantime, our manager, Mr Vinod Phadke, organized a beachside barbeque dinner for us.

On the semi-final day we entered the field with great enthusiasm. We were playing against England as they had topped their group. And phew! Once again I lost the toss. The coach was disappointed but the toss is always something beyond a captain's control. What I would be able to control was the fate of the match. We were put in first and their bowling fireworks began. We lost early wickets and were straight away under pressure. Manan was caught when we were 30, Akhil followed at 48; Zol was gone at 70, while Nath ran himself out when we reached 105. At 108, Aparajith was caught and bowled. We were five down then. I was standing at one end and the pressure was building. It was real pressure. I could feel it on me. I was trying to take deep breaths not to succumb to it.

Smit Patel joined me and we were very careful. I was beaten on quite a few occasions but still kept going. We were slow but that day wickets mattered more than runs. I knew that if we could bat the full overs, we could put up a decent total. We were building a good partnership. As a batsman, it is really important to hang in there even when you get beaten numerous times and cut a sorry figure. That's only a temporary phase. Once set you can turn the tables, which is what I managed to do that day. Slowly, I started opening up. The fours started coming and the sixes too. I hit six fours and four sixes, and ended up scoring 94. I got out trying to hit another six, caught at the sweeper boundary. I could have stayed there for some more time as there were still six overs left in our innings. Smit was an able partner and scored 53. He is a tough guy and almost always performs under pressure. He plays his best when someone pushes him, goads him and talks to him while at the crease. I was always there for him, walking down to him, talking to him, scolding and encouraging him after every ball. We had a partnership of 90 runs. He was to do the same thing in the World Cup final too.

We were bowled out for 239 in 49.1 overs. Now all we needed was the support of our bowlers, and they were bang on. I always vouch for video analysis as it really helps. The night before the match, we had watched their batting visuals and marked the areas where they scored the most. For instance, we had plans for their main batsman Drummond, and executed them perfectly. We just bowled to him outside off, never letting him score square of the wicket. He struggled and we got him quickly. Sandy took some early wickets. Things heated up between the two sides as Sandy and Harry started sledging two Indian players in the English side. The umpire had to finally stop them as the situation could have worsened. The feeling of revenge that we nursed proved quite effective for us; we really meant business and it showed in our body language. Every one of us was putting pressure on the English boys. All the fielders in the circle would come right up to the batsman after each delivery, chirping in their ears, making life difficult for them in the middle. Finally, our aggression and enthusiasm paid off. They lost six wickets for 65. We did not let them even touch 200. Their innings folded at 176 and we won by 63 runs. What a moment! Now we were ready and confident for the final. The news from the other ground was that Australia had beaten New Zealand, so we would face them in the final.

So there we were, in the final of the quadrangular series for the second time, having won the first at home, seven-nil. There was talk that Pat Cummins would be playing the final for Australia. Cummins had already represented his national Test side and had done brilliantly. He had been the main destroyer during the Australia–South Africa Test series a few months earlier. So, as a team, we now had something to talk about. We kept pulling each other's legs. How were we going to face him? Facing a ball hurled at you 150 km per hour on an Australian pitch is no joke. Our batsmen were the main target of banter. '*Bhai, Cummins khel raha hai kal,*' I told Manan and he smiled drily. Jokes apart, I was myself concerned about Cummins; he was going to be their main weapon. I decided that the best thing would be to just see him through.

It was toss time again. Writing these lines I'm so relaxed because I know the outcome of the match, but standing on the pitch that day, my heart was really beating hard. Everyone of us was praying for the coin to fall in our favour. I called 'tails' and as soon as the coin landed I saw tails smiling at me. I jumped with joy! The excitement was not because it would help us win but because this was the only front where I was being defeated time and again. Winning the toss for the first time was a good omen. Very sure of my decision, I elected to bowl. I found the wicket slightly damp, which would make life difficult for the Australian batsmen.

The excitement and the feel of fielding first as well as the increased chance of winning made all of us go crazy. Right from the word go, we ran around the field with tremendous energy; we were really on top of our game. While the fielding was top-notch, our bowling attack again rose to the occasion. It is really important for a team to excel on all fronts—batting, bowling and fielding. That's how it can win matches consistently.

Australia were four down for 78. Sandy was on fire—he took four wickets. Harmeet also bowled well. We restricted them to 194, not a difficult target to chase. But I knew it was important that I finish the game myself as some of our batsmen were not in the best frame of mind. Our batsmen had a silly tendency to fall in quick succession. They appeared quite unreliable at times.

Manan and Akhil opened the innings. Pat was bowling really quick. Akhil was his first victim and we were one down on 17 when I went in to bat. The Aussies really tore into me—they were relentless in their sledging. We lost Manan soon. Manan had been playing well. But despite my telling him to take it easy against Pat, he went after him and got caught. Both the wickets fell to Pat. The sledging only made me even more determined. I was feeling confident and strong within. It took me some time to adjust to Pat's pace. He skids the ball, so it looks as if the speed is normal, but you end up in a precarious position. His ball comes very quickly through the air and speeds up after hitting the deck. My plan was to see him off. Even though I had spent seven overs at the crease by that point, I still felt under a lot of pressure.

I vividly remember that day. It was cloudy while we were batting and I was sweating profusely. I was very clear in my mind about my role, probably because the responsibility was now solely mine. I used to tell all the batsmen how to go about their innings, and would even admonish them at times to play in a particular way. Now I was following exactly what I preached. All that I said had come naturally from within me. Guiding them, I also discovered myself. I may find it difficult to repeat it now, but all through my Under-19 years, I was adept at shouldering responsibility. This helped me to discover my approach to the game and widened my horizons. My game is very much like Manan's; I am also a natural stroke player. So anything in my range is dispatched to the boundary and that was what happened in this innings.

I ended up hitting Pat for two long sixes, thereby finishing his spell. Afterwards, life was easy in the middle. In games where you have experienced and quick bowlers like Pat Cummins, other bowlers look relatively easy once you've seen off the big guys. I could easily manoeuvre the other bowlers all around the park. In matches with low targets, it is only a matter of a couple of good partnerships and then the match becomes one sided. Akshdeep and I were the two who finished it off. Akshdeep can play all around the park. He is equally good at singles and sixes. This guy can really hit the ball hard. I've always had confidence in him. His attitude is infectious on the field; it's fun batting with him. During this partnership, we joked around, which really eased the pressure. We milked their attack, a very special feeling indeed.

I had tried to remain calm while batting. But one bowler, Harry Conway, was coming far too close to me. Not just that, every time he came close, he would mutter a few bad words too. I decided to go after him. I looked for a length ball and as soon as I got one, it went flying over the rope. I hit him for another six soon. I ended up hitting six sixes in my unbeaten innings of 112. This was going to be exactly the same number of sixes that I hit in the World Cup final too. We won the match emphatically. The Aussies beaten by seven wickets!

It was party time! We didn't booze but definitely had soft drinks and sprayed them on everyone in the dressing room. Everyone was soaked in the revelry, and we really messed up the dressing room. Love and bonding increase many folds when a team wins such matches and tournaments. We kept hugging each other. It was crazy. The worst part was that we had to vacate the ground as early as possible because we had an early evening flight to Brisbane—we were flying back to India from Brisbane the next morning.

This was our second tournament win on the trot. The best thing was the venue of the tournament. The U-19 World Cup was scheduled to be held at the same place, in Townsville. Who knew at that time that history was going to be repeated here and we were going to beat Australia again, in the final of the U-19 World Cup at the same venue, on 26 August 2012.

On our way back to the airport, we had lots of fun in the bus. It had been a good trip; we'd made some good friends there. Mano di and Harjinder paaji had become like family to us there. Every evening, the boys used to go to their house for delicious dinners. Mano di always had sweets ready for us. Then there was this Gujarati boy, Shashank Kodesia, who became a dear friend of mine and with whom I used to hang out a lot. He took me to all the happening places in Townsville and never missed an opportunity to enrich me with his wise words. Another person with whom the team became friendly was John, a local Indian who helped us in every possible way. He also invited the entire team to dinner at his place. Both these guys really made us feel at home in Australia. It's difficult to find such generous people. The intimacy has strengthened over time and when the WC came, we had already become a family.

6

In the Big League

It's not about being better than someone else;
it's about being better than you were the day before.

—Unknown

The Indian Premier League has its admirers and critics. Even after five seasons of IPL, people are discussing whether it is good or bad for the game. Experts have gone on record to claim that T20 cricket is ruining young players. Their logic is that a player has to learn to be a Test cricketer first, instead of which he now starts playing in the IPL, which is nothing but bang-bang cricket. They may or may not be right. But it cannot be denied that the IPL has had a huge impact on cricket. For some players, it has been a stage to showcase their talents, while for some others the going has been extremely tough—it all depends on how you take it.

The IPL has been a great learning experience for me. If I look back at my three years in the league, my first season with the Delhi Daredevils turned out to be a baptism by fire. I vividly remember I was preparing for my Class XII board exams when the call came. Obviously, it was a big day for me. The IPL had already completed three successful seasons and was preparing for the fourth one. It had changed people's perception of and expectations from cricket. All they wanted to see was a T20 game flooded with fours and sixes, and the glamour quotient that came with it. Now no one on the streets asked me when I would be a part of the Indian team; all they asked was whether I was playing in the IPL or not. Fair enough. So when the big news came, it quickly spread around. It was a great feeling. Though I wasn't sure if I would be getting any matches to play that season, I wanted to practise all those fancy shots, and keep hitting sixes in the nets. But I had my exams too to be taken care of; so I had to sit at home and study. My franchisees were kind enough to grant me leave from practice sessions whenever I wanted it.

It was a great feeling to be a part of that group. And

then the big thing happened. We played a practice match among ourselves and I scored an unbeaten 60 off 40 balls. In the next practice match I scored 49 off 20 balls, even hitting James Hopes (the Australian all-rounder) for 20 runs in one over. Soon, the whole perception about me changed. I was looked at as a key player and there was talk of playing me in the very first match. I remember Aashish Kapoor sir (the manager) calling me a day before the first match and informing me to be ready for the game against the Mumbai Indians. He said, 'Take your parents' blessings, you are playing tomorrow.' My heart skipped a beat. My breathing became shallow. I lost my appetite. I felt too full of everything. On hearing the good news from the manager, I called my uncle, my coach and a few close friends. I was unable to study after the news came in. I was lost in dreams and fantasies. I started dreaming of that moment when I would enter the ground, and enthral one and all with my heroic hitting.

Diary Entry
6 April 2011

Just two days are left for the mega event we all had been waiting for. The IPL will be celebrating its fourth birthday on 8th April. But this time things have slightly changed for me. Till now I have grown up watching it, enjoying each moment of it, supporting sides, even betting with my friends, and loving the whole campaign and always wishing to be part of it someday. And now the time has come. I feel so awesome being a part of the Delhi Daredevils, but at the same time I am quite wary of what's going to happen. I remember last year when Delhi was playing against Mumbai at the Feroz Shah Kotla, I had gone through so much trouble to get passes for the match. My mother and I were sitting at the stands, and I was wondering when I would get to play.

You really become a part of the team you are supporting. Its victory is your victory and its defeat becomes yours. Everything is so easy when you are a spectator. You go out there to cheer, chill, have fun and enjoy the three hours of game-time. But hardly anyone puts themselves in the players' shoes. The spectators feel that these stars are lucky to be there, earning handsome money and enjoying the fame; they fail to recognize their hard work and the pressure they have to deal with—pressure to perform from their franchises, spectators, media, and especially from within themselves. It's rightly said that if you are there at the top, then the whole world is with you, idolizes you, but once you show a slight slump you are criticized, you almost become a nobody. Fortunes change faster in cricket than in any other sport.

A year has passed since I watched the match at Kotla between Mumbai and Delhi as a spectator. But now, after four days (on 10 April 2011), I may be playing my first match against the mighty Mumbai Indians! I still can't believe it is for real. It feels great that I have been able to make some progress and have reached the next level of my cricketing journey. But at the same time my heart beats even faster when I imagine myself playing against Sachin and facing Malinga at the same Kotla grounds where I had sat and cheered for Delhi Daredevils last year. This time I cannot occupy that seat. Tomorrow is my last board exam and that too of psychology. But here I am sitting at my study table and writing this diary, not able to concentrate and just dreaming of the big day. I have been having goosebumps all day, especially whenever I start thinking about the match. I'm nervous, I'm scared, I'm apprehensive, I'm excited, I'm impatient—I am exploding with feelings. I have no idea what it is going to be like when I enter the field with the players I have always idolized. I mean I started playing cricket watching them. My hands have started trembling again. But I know it will be great to be in the place I had always dreamt of being in, and things are happening for me. These feelings are bound to arise. I bet Sachin felt the same way twenty-one years ago. This is how it has to be. So I am cool.

There are a few other things that are also exciting me. Among those are shoots, security briefings, promotional events, and mug shots for various purposes. This all sounds like, 'Oh, my god! It is really happening!' I feel elated when these things happen. We had our shoots for the hoardings they are going to put across the city; we had meetings with the franchisees; then team meetings and practice matches, security briefings about movements in and around the hotel and stadium, about security at the hotel, with a convoy of armed police patrolling us . . . I can't believe it!

People from the anti-corruption bureau had also come to brief us about the incidents that have occurred in the past and given cricket a bad name, and how they could be prevented. The illegal system of betting and fixing was also discussed and they explained the sources through which the bookies can approach and influence us.

This is international stuff; I am soon going to enter the world of glamour where everyone will be following you. Everyone will be watching you. Responsibility increases. It is now for me to learn to handle the expectations, pressures, and everything that comes with it like a professional.

This is the beginning of my career and I have to make it BIG. Is it really happening?!

I vividly remember that first match against Mumbai Indians. Everyone was excited before the match. As was part of my superstitious ritual, I could be found by my favourite gods, praying for a good start. All my bats were lined up at the mandir of my house. I was preparing my weapons for a solid explosion. Mom applied tika on my forehead and on all the bats, and sent me to 'war'. (Dad himself drove me to ITC Maurya, the hotel where our team was staying.) Later on, I began to feel that you should never do different things like these just prior to such events because they make you feel that you are doing something special, and it builds the whole thing up and stresses you out. You should just follow your normal daily routine. It gets you more in sync with your preparations. In the meanwhile, I made all the important calls to close friends and relatives to remind them to keep their TV sets on in the evening.

After a round of photos we gathered for the team meeting in the hotel, where I was officially told about my inclusion in the side for the match. Everyone congratulated me. My stress levels rose considerably. I could feel the nerves coming back. We entered the team bus taking our usual positions as a matter of habit or you could call it superstition, though I don't usually believe in this. I sat next to the window and tried to enjoy the feeling, though my mind was stuck on how I would play. I think it's really important to enjoy every moment that comes your way: the tough times, the struggles, the failures, the disappointments, the doubts, and finally the little success that lightens up your spirits and bolsters you for the same set of motions all over again. When you look back, you realize the fun is always in the journey.

After winning the World Cup, newer challenges, and fresh aims and goals had come up. I remember the preparatory camps that were held to get the team in shape. Although there were so many doubts, and ifs and buts, the aim was clear. I strongly think that if you are committed to something with your full heart and soul in it, your belief becomes so strong that achieving the result itself becomes a given. Today when I write this, I am in that stage of doubt where I don't know what will happen next. Though honestly speaking, I have no doubts about my future—I really mean it.

On that journey to the stadium for the first match, I was still dreaming. It was a rare moment; I thanked god for giving me the opportunity to see how it feels to be cheered for. The passers-by couldn't stop waving at the team bus and trying to catch a glimpse of their favourite stars. It was unreal to see so many people queued up to see us play and cheer for us! Sometimes I feel lucky to be a cricketer—we are paid for doing something we love, and people love us for hitting fours and sixes. Insane!

The dressing room was a happy place to be in. Everyone was getting ready and getting into their zones, following their routines, whether it meant listening to music or relaxing on their chairs. The Kotla dressing room gives a good view of the whole ground. I was just standing in the balcony and watching things, trying to adapt to the crowd. I like to observe a lot. In the dressing rooms too, I keep watching the players and make a mental note of what they are doing. It's fun.

I entered the ground all too conscious of myself. I could not get into the focused blank zone. As I felt I was being watched, my actions were no longer natural or spontaneous. We won the toss and elected to bat. I was given the no. 3 slot. Sehwag and Warner went in. There were deafening roars and Mexican waves, and blue-and-red flags swamped the Kotla. The atmosphere was electrifying. Before I could put myself into the match situation, Warner was bowled by the famous Malinga yorker. It was my turn to face the music now. What was I thinking? Well, nothing. For the first time in my life, I went in to bat without a plan because I didn't know what was happening. While I was walking to the crease, I could visualize myself being seen on the TV screens, the reactions of my friends and family members. I hadn't got into match mode or perhaps I wasn't fully prepared for the occasion. I was nervous while facing the first ball. It was a full toss from Malinga which I somehow defended and the bat twisted in my hands. At that level, your reactions can reveal your state of mind to the opposition. Mine was an eye-opening reaction—I was totally at sea. My reaction after that first ball was probably something like: 'Oh yeah, that was quick, good morning, buddy, wake up, you need to be quicker than that.' I expected Malinga to bowl to me even faster after my first response, to intimidate and scare me, but the opposite happened. He bowled a slower one to which my bat automatically moved faster due to the previous ball on my mind. I didn't know what I was trying to do. Maybe I was trying to make a bold statement saying that I had arrived. I swung my bat at it so hard that I missed the ball and it crashed into my wickets, which landed 10 yards back. I could see Malinga pumping his fists in the air and laughing at the way he had fooled me. Game over! I had become an easy victim. On my way back to the pavilion, I was careful about not showing my emotions to the camera. Did I really need to be so conscious? All I can say is that I was totally oblivious to my surroundings. I knew that this shouldn't have happened, but that's how you learn. I had been told beforehand of similar things, but actually being a part of such a situation was something entirely different. Nothing brings the point home like experiencing it. I learned the hard way. It wasn't that I didn't want to get into the zone; I just wasn't able to find the zone.

So my first IPL innings was eminently forgettable, but I will always remember the delight of playing against the great Sachin Tendulkar, my hero.

Diary Entry
11 April 2011

PLAYING AGAINST SACHIN

Playing against Sachin was a very special moment for me. Though I got out early I very carefully watched him bat. The first thing I noticed was that playing late is a dominant trait of a successful batsman. Sachin really plays very late. He has more than one answer to every delivery. He has the ability to manoeuvre the ball 360 degrees. The thing about him that surprised me was that he knew what the next ball would be. That is how well prepared he is. Another jaw-dropping (literally) aspect of his batting was the way he was hitting the ball. I could compare it to a boxer punching his opponent's face. The science involved in punching hard is to exhale when you punch. I could feel Sachin doing the same when driving and punching. He had time, he would get into the correct position and then whack the ball hard while exhaling in a relaxed manner. He must have put in loads of practice to reach that level of perfection he has achieved. This inspires me. These days when I go out to bat and get tired, those images of Sachin come to my mind, telling me: 'Sachin is too far and high, but if I keep going, I'll get one step closer to him.'

And that's how my IPL began. A zero in my first match was followed by two in the second one against Rajasthan Royals. But I was in better control of myself in the second outing although I played a maiden over—which is not the best thing to do in a T20 match.

I'm still learning but over these couple of years I have learned that T20 is not about hitting every ball. It's a technical and smart game. People keep saying that T20 is a major cause behind flawed techniques. But I like to think that T20 is a very technical game. As a batsman, I can give it in writing that a player with improper technique cannot succeed in T20 at the international level. You cannot clear the boundary consistently against top-class bowlers. To succeed in doing so, it's really important to have a strong base and a decent technique. T20 is never about hitting the ball hard and clearing the fence; it will never be so. Playing the ball late and staying in control are the key factors. I don't want to get into the intricacies of T20 here, but I definitely want my readers to know my view about this format and how I myself have adapted to it over the years and the impact it has had on me so far.

In the T20s, I have now shifted slightly towards playing a normal game. That said, I must confess it's never easy to play your natural game in a T20. You always look to overdo and that's when problem arises. Now I try to focus more on my breathing patterns and keeping a check on my sudden impulses. This is easier said than done, especially in a game like cricket of which everyone seems to be an expert, wherein they give you detailed responses to the questions you throw at them.

The IPL has helped me a lot. When I compare the player that I was two years ago to the player that I am now, things have changed a lot. And the IPL has definitely made a positive contribution to that change. I couldn't have imagined sharing dressing rooms, hotel rooms and the same stage with such big stars at such a young age. It has given me tremendous exposure, which otherwise wouldn't have been possible till the time I played for the country. For the very first time, I actually saw and felt the reality of the pressure that international cricket entails. It is overwhelming, and it really helped me understand how I would need to develop to be able to handle it when I played U-19 cricket. If it weren't for the IPL, I would have felt the intensity of the pressure only when I was actually playing the U-19 World Cup matches where I would have been facing it for the first time.

It's not only about the dressing room but also about the time we spent together. For someone of my age, then eighteen, getting to interact and asking questions of the best in business was a big thing. I've learned so much from them. I mean, you practise with them, you watch their work ethics on the field, you meet them off the field, and slowly you start imbibing their healthy traits and try fitting them into your system. This definitely makes a difference. Someone living in a healthy atmosphere becomes healthier; and it's always good to be infected with a positive attitude.

Cricket is a sport where experience counts, and the IPL has given me a lot of exposure, which has definitely helped me in my Under-19 feats. More than your game, it's your level of confidence that matters. In my case, being the only U-19 player to have played in the IPL, and also because I was a regular in the Ranji squad, helped boost my confidence and belief that I could lead the Indian U-19 side. I was respected by my U-19 teammates because they acknowledged my achievements, thereby making it easier for me to captain them. I can say that playing the IPL, and Ranji has helped me cope with the pressures of the game. At times I have felt at ease in situations where my buddies felt pressured.

In a nutshell, the IPL has helped me evolve. I now have a better understanding of the game and its situations. So I credit IPL and Ranji for improving my game, and sincerely hope that they will teach me more in the coming years and make me a better player.

7

When Arch-rivals Meet

Victory belongs to the most persevering.

—Napoleon

I have heard people say that there is too much cricket, and it's having a negative effect on players. They lose form, lose the hunger for runs, get injured too often, and become complacent. But this has never been the case with me. Perhaps I am too young to be bothered by it. In fact, the more I play, the more I enjoy myself. Too much cricket is never an excuse for me. It's my profession and I love it more than anything else. I feel good that I am busy playing different tournaments in different conditions against different teams. It gives me valuable experience. It's always fun going to new places, venues and countries to play cricket. I had already visited two cricket-playing countries and now was the time for the third: Malaysia. The Under-19 Asia Cup was to be held in Kuala Lumpur.

Needless to mention, the atmosphere in the camp was full of excitement. Our camaraderie was improving and the focus was shifting from individuals to the team. We all knew that we were going to play against Pakistan for the first time. I don't know why playing against Pakistan has a special feeling. Maybe it's because of the historic rivalry between the twins separated at birth.

Malaysia is 'truly Asia', and very similar to India— only the number of high-rise buildings are an exception. People there are more law abiding, although I've heard that pickpocketing and chain snatching are rather common there, so one needs to be alert while on the streets. Malaysia also has places where clothes and electronic goods can be bought cheap, much like Gaffar Market and Palika Bazaar of Delhi. But honestly, I didn't like going to these places. Most of us struggled to find good stuff, except Harmeet who is very fond of perfumes and took a bagful of them. We told him not to bother but he wouldn't listen and he went on his shopping spree. He could have found the same things in Mumbai as well. Watching him, the others, including myself, changed our minds and decided to buy a few things. We'd all talked so much about the cheap electronic goods available in Malaysia that all of us had planned to buy LCD TVs, but eventually we were all lost in the excitement of cricket and came back home empty-handed—except, of course, for the coveted trophy.

All our matches were held at the Kinrara Oval, except the one against Nepal. Kinrara Oval is the same ground where India won the U-19 World Cup in 2008 under Virat Kohli's captaincy. Most of us had watched the match on TV; we were trying to recollect the moments of the match and how they celebrated after winning it. When you are playing a tournament like the Asia Cup, you know that there are only a few tough teams, as the rest of them, like Malaysia, Nepal and Afghanistan, are easy rivals. Cricket is new to them and they are still striving for proper infrastructure. Perhaps in a few years they will build up good teams, but at the time they were comparatively weak. Still, it would have been foolish of us to underestimate any of our opponents. It doesn't take much time for things to change in a cricket match. But it's really difficult to keep your mental focus and concentration when playing against weak opposition. You tend to become casual and that's when you get out cheaply—which is exactly what happened to me: 38 against Malaysia and 48 against Nepal.

Getting out against these teams really killed me and I sulked badly. I felt I had missed out on a couple of big opportunities to score big. Our group was a relatively easy one. Only the match with Pakistan had the potential to be a good battle and it definitely turned out to be one.

Playing against Pakistan is special

Though the media and the public make much of India–Pakistan matches, initially I did not have any special feeling regarding the match. It was just another match for me. But the crowd that turned up for our match against Pakistan! It was really huge. Flags were waved and slogans shouted! As the match progressed, the atmosphere got more and more electrifying. I was actually scared. Playing first, Pakistan scored 287 for 7. Rush Kalaria bowled well to take four wickets. I was very confident of chasing down the target. But once again I could not convert my start to a big one and got out on 49. But Zol was in his element that day and Nath supported him very well. It turned out to be a very tight finish. We needed two runs to win off the last ball but it was not to be. Mohsin played a shot but Zol did not go for the run. Imagine, the last ball of the match and you are not going for the run! If Zol had gone for the run, we would have tied the match. We lost it by just one run. Zol really got it from me. I was very upset. It took some time for me to be normal again. But as we had anyway qualified, the let-down did not last long.

For me, while winning is important, learning from the previous match and properly planning for the next is even more important. As we were constantly reminded by our beloved coaches, debriefing after the match is as important as planning before the match. Debriefing helps you to realize how things shaped up in a match and what could have been done to improve the result, and what corrections should be made if we face that particular situation again. It helps you to prepare well; honestly, it has done wonders for me.

It was fun off the field. Almost everyone partied in Malaysia, except those under eighteen: Zol, Akhil and Aparajith. I have not seen a guy as simple as Aparajith. Oh, man! He sleeps at nine. No girlfriends, no parties, never seen him hyper; he's always smiling and down to earth. He is a different character altogether, but a great buddy and team man. I will tell you about all my teammates towards the end of the book.

By this time I could feel a strong bond developing amongst us. I realized that this phase was never going to come back again. The next two months would be our last two months together as a team, after which we would probably face each other in domestic contests. Some players would definitely play for their state teams, while others might not. Some of them might even make it big. But one thing was certain: this dream Under-19 team would never play together again after the World Cup. Such fleeting thoughts made me very emotional at times. Most of us had been together for the past three years. We had seen each other grow. We had had issues amongst us, which were eventually sorted out. Guys with whom I hated to talk are the ones with whom I hang out the most now. This whole team had become a family and as a captain I often felt proud—this is my team! I had never experienced this sense of belonging in any other teams that I had played for until then. I was ready to give everything for this team's success. It was a wonderful lot of highly talented youngsters. But there cannot be a family without guardians. We were really lucky to have such great mentors in Bharath sir, Sridhar sir, Sudarshan sir, Srinivasan sir and Sanju sir. They are the best people to have as coaches-cum-friends—solid cricket enthusiasts with impeccable knowledge and tactical brilliance. They bonded the team very well.

In the huddle before the semi-final of the Asia Cup against Sri Lanka, I told my boys about this familial feeling I had discovered. They were really charged up and everyone wanted to back the members of the family. We started off really well. We restricted them to 84 in 24 overs, but a late partnership gave them a fighting total of 295. It was a humid day. Fielding first for 50 overs and then batting for the same amount of time gave me some jitters. But that is how cricket is played. I have been doing this for so many years now that it has become a routine.

During the innings break I freshened up, took a cold shower, lay down for a while and then went in to bat. I knew it was very important for me to stay till the end as it wasn't an easy chase and required some amount of patience and maturity. Now I am proud to say I accomplished my goal. There were a few goosebumps around the late 40s because of my previous failures at that stage. It was a great relief to cross the 50 mark. And after that there was no stopping me. I got my third hundred for India in youth ODIs. By god's grace it came at the perfect time. We won the match rather comfortably. I just hoped that I carried my form further in the final against Pakistan too.

The final battle

If you look at the history of one-day cricket, there are only a few tied matches. A tie is the ultimate result one can expect in a one-day match. Nothing can beat it. Equal score at the end of 50 overs! The anxiety, swinging fortunes of both the teams, increasing heartbeats, the superstitions, fans not changing their positions—it had all the ingredients of a super-exciting final. I've written the story of that heart-thumping final in my diary:

Diary Entry
1 July 2012

India playing against Pakistan in the final of the Asia Cup! What more could cricket lovers ask for? A lot of buzz has been going around about the final. My parents were also very excited and tense. Despite my resentment of their never-ending free advice and do's and don'ts, they could not resist instructing me and trying to help me out (according to them) for the big match. My uncle has a habit of writing long letters with do's and don'ts before big tournaments and matches. My father does all sorts of research on the strengths and weaknesses of the opposition players, and both he and my uncle came out with a strategy for the opposition that I should apply as captain. At times their advice has helped me and enriched my thought process. But I believe in instincts in on-field situations. My mother sometimes just goes insane. She is so nervous that she goes to sleep and can't muster the courage to watch me live. But whenever she gets hold of me on the phone it becomes really very difficult to stop her. She also comes out with so many this-and-that I could have done. Sometimes I really get pissed off. But it's OK. It just shows how concerned they are about me. And then there is the overwhelming wave of patriotism. Since we were playing against Pakistan, many of my friends and relatives connected it to nationalism and patriotism. Their SMSs were all full of such feeling.

All this was happening outside. But the atmosphere in the dressing room was completely different. We were having fun. We just had a very brief meeting yesterday and it was more friendly banter than a formal meeting. I had a busy day yesterday. I went shopping and had a gourmet's delight for dinner with the father of my close friend Utsav who happened to be there for some work and was staying in the same hotel. We all chilled out. For us it was just another match, though I was very excited and raring to go.

To begin with, I got to the team bus ten minutes late, courtesy my mobile's dead battery. We reached the ground and started with our routines. Kinrara Oval is a batting paradise, but because of our previous successful chases, we opted to field after winning the toss. We started really well. We were able to contain the runs, but suddenly the momentum changed and drifted towards Pakistanis. At one point it looked as if they were going to score 300-plus runs. But a superb second spell by Rush Kalaria in the death overs brought us back into the game. Pakistan scored 283.

There were huge numbers of Indian and Pakistani

spectators who had come to support their teams. Looking at them I could make out that it had become a matter of pride for them. They wanted to establish, through the result of the match, the supremacy of one over the other. They were more thrilled, and competed with each other much more aggressively than the players on the ground. They went berserk at the fall of a wicket and shouted at every boundary. Pakistan's supporters were screaming out their religious songs and slogans. The Indians too were completely soaked in revelry with their dhols and songs.

The target of 283 was a big one, but very much achievable on this wicket, provided we batted with discipline and determination. My contribution had to be crucial and I knew that I had to stay at the crease till the end. I knew my plan and just wanted to repeat what I had done in the semi-final against Sri Lanka. Pakistan's pace attack was impressive. I tried to see off the opening spell with caution. But runs kept flowing. Manan got out early but Baba Aparajith filled in his shoes really well. He supported me brilliantly from the other end. And eventually we started dominating them without taking any big risks. The wicket was a good one for batting and the ball was coming onto the bat nicely. We just had to guide it into the gaps. We did a good job and added over 150 runs for the second wicket. I knew it was very important to finish the game myself as it doesn't take time for momentum to shift in a cricket match. But Baba's wicket was a huge blow. He played a fantastic knock of 90 before getting out. I told myself to be patient. Now the Pakistani bowlers were coming at us very hard. Their body language had changed. I scored my century in the 43rd over.

We were just three wickets down and only 37 more runs were required. I was calm from within though I could sense trouble brewing as wickets started falling from the other end. But I kept on scoring runs without indulging in anything fancy. My plan was to take the team as close as possible to the target. But luck would not favour me. I was caught at the cover boundary on the fourth ball of the final over. We needed five runs in the last two balls. Rush Kalaria hit a four to tie the score. But he could only chip to a waiting fielder off the final ball, a dot. And the match was tied, leaving the Indian supporters stunned. I was furious with myself. But that was momentary.

I realized that there was no point in persisting with my anger—at least we had tied and not lost. And we had learned an important lesson about digging in. In hindsight, if we had won or lost the Asia Cup, we might have been overconfident or diffident during the World Cup. The Asia Cup was like a semi-final on our way to the final destination: the World Cup.

Twinkle, twinkle, little star: Little Unmukt perched on dad Bharat Chand Thakur's shoulders.

Shot! Learning the ropes at Lovely Park, Mayur Vihar, New Delhi.

Light burden: At the National Stadium, Delhi.

In familiar company: At home.

Uncle's blessing: With uncle Sunder Chand Thakur after making it to the Delhi Under-15 team.

Disciple and Guru: With coach Sanjay Bhardwaj.

Big-match player: After the century against Pakistan in the final of the Asia Cup at Kuala Lumpur, 2012. Photo © AP

The adventure gene: Rappelling at the boot camp before the U-19 World Cup.

A happy picture: After a century, and victory against the Aussies in the final of the quadrangular series in Australia, 2012.

Tip and run: On his way to a maiden Ranji century.

Career climb: Batting with Shikhar Dhawan against Gujarat while making his Ranji debut.

A study in balance: Batting for the Delhi Daredevils in IPL-6.
Photo © Sportzpics/IPL

One for the album: Posing with Virendra Sehwag.

Tips from the Master: Listening to Sir Vivian Richards.
Photo © Delhi Daredevils

The learning curve: All ears and eyes to Mahela Jayawardene.
Photo © Delhi Daredevils

Honours from the Little Master: Receiving the CEAT Indian Youngster of the Year Award, 2012, from Sunil Gavaskar. Photo © CEAT Cricket Rating

Youth Icon: Speaking at 'Mind Rocks', the India Today Youth Conclave, 2012. Photo © India Today

Warm home: With dad, Bharat Chand Thakur, and mom, Rajeshwari Chand.
Photo © V.V. Krishnan

The sky is the limit: At Pengong Lake in Leh with friends Arjun (centre) and
Utsav (right).

A hero's arrival: In a chariot on his way home after winning the World Cup.

Champions! Celebration time after the U-19 World Cup triumph.
Photo © ICC/Getty Images

PART II

THE WORLD CUP

8

The Team

To handle yourself, use your head;
to handle others, use your heart.

—Eleanor Roosevelt

There we were. On the way to the World Cup. By this point we had become one close-knit family—the players and the support staff. We were raring to go! But then disaster struck. Manan injured his finger, and Mohsin was struck by malaria just a few days before our journey. So we left for Australia with two new people in the squad. Even so, we were still a family, and I spent so much time with my team that, by the time we won the championship, I knew everyone inside out. And I want you to know all of them too, as they all played equally important roles in making us the champions. Then there are my mentors and coaches who have trained and counselled and encouraged me from the very start. Every one of these people had their role to play in us winning the World Cup and me becoming the person and the cricketer I am today. Here they are!

Smit Patel

I'll start with Smit Patel. The mere thought of Smit always makes me break into a smile—no, more than a smile, it makes me laugh out of sheer joy. Smit Kamlesh Patel, the '*NRI ke bacche*' (as we all called him), is a good buddy. Sometimes, I felt sorry for this Gujarati boy because we always pulled his leg. We would tease him so much that he used to say he wouldn't want to see us again after the tournament was done! But I bet he would love to be back among the guys. Often he would feel frustrated by our pranks on him, especially Sandy's. But he would routinely do things that got him into trouble. Smit is a unique character, one of a kind. He was always in Hollister trousers and T-shirts. That was his trademark, as if he was its brand ambassador. In his room, he would be roaming around in funky, colourful trousers. I have seen him wandering in hotel corridors in high pyjamas.

On the field, again, he cut a different picture. He would have way too much zinc on his face and on the rest of exposed skin, while his eyes were protected by sunglasses. He was always giving us opportunities to pull his leg.

We used to also tease him for his strange voice and pronunciation. His voice sounded like a cuckoo, and a Gujarati one at that! Although he constantly travelled to the US (his family is based there), his accent was very much Indian. Alarm for him was 'A-la-ram'. I still tease him with that. I know once he reads these lines, he will kill me. Smitya! Buddy, it's out of my love for you that I am sharing all this. Please don't get angry. I know by now you would have already turned red. Literally, guys! Smit would always turn red when it was hot outside or if he felt dejected. He is indeed a great friend. I miss those moments when we batted together, miss those long partnerships we shared at crucial junctures. And what great temperament you displayed in the grand final. I was so worried and constantly approached you to tell you to just hang in there. And you did it, Smitya. Let me tell you that you are a top-class batsman, a match winner and a brilliant wicketkeeper. You have it all in you. The *jazbati* guy that you are will take you to greater glory. You are a great prospect for the country and I wish you luck for the future. Now you should not turn red, NRI ke bachche!

Harmeet Singh

Then there's Harmeet Singh. Harry, the great Khalsa, and my off-field companion, is a damn cool guy, quite relaxed and has a great sense of style. He shops a lot. He likes to spend on himself but doesn't at all mind spending on friends too. He has a big heart and stays away from petty things. He has a great sense of humour and laughs the way a Sardarji should actually laugh—long and loud. And boy, can he dance! It's like his legs just move without him thinking about it.

It took us some time to get to know each other properly. We didn't start off too close—we'd been in rival teams since the days of U-15 cricket—but eventually, our relationship got better. We spent a lot of time off-field together and explored new places. Harry is a prankster. He has a dominating presence. A crucial member of our team, he always tried to contribute, not just through his bowling and batting, but also through valuable advice. His suggestions helped me a lot.

Of course, I cannot forget his bowling heroics. He is a top-class spinner. Ian Chappell has praised him, and many others too have expressed their views about his potential as a great spinner. He is a team man, and can contribute with the bat as well. He is also known for hitting big sixes. Who can forget his knock against Pakistan in the quarter-final of the World Cup? He got us back into the match with his superb batting. He is a rescuer. Harry is the perfect combo of Mumbai and Punjabi cultures. He has just bought a black XUV 500, and looks even more dashing driving that giant, dressed in black from head to toe. He is a rock star. Keep soaring high, Daarji!

Baba Aparajith

Baba Aparajith is the quintessential 'good boy' of our group, with exceptional skills and abundant talent. I have never seen someone more grounded and sweet. He is probably the most disciplined and well mannered amongst us. I can't remember seeing him outside his room after 9 p.m. even once. He never parties. In fact, at times, I have pushed him to come with us at night. Then he'd ask me if the whole team was going (including the support staff). If not, there was no chance I could drag him with me, whatever the occasion.

Though we had been together for two years, I don't know that much about him because we have never really hung out off the field. I do know that he is basically an introvert, a shy guy. This adds to his simplicity. He is neither too aggressive nor too docile. He always maintains a calm demeanour. If you ask me, I think he's the best cricketer amongst us. His batting technique is rock solid and elegant, and his temperament really sound. He was our wall, our Rahul Dravid. You just have to admire his batting— everything in line, the head, shoulders, body behind the ball, the right head-to-toe movement and then the smooth downswing of the bat, hitting the ball right under the nose. He is a perfect copybook player.

And let's not forget that his offspin is as lethal as his batting. The way he flights the ball in the air, many a batsman has fallen prey to him. He was one of our top wicket-takers in the Under-19 tournaments. He bowled magical spells in the quadrangular series in Vizag. We had actually started treating him more as a bowler than as a batsman. And he is a top-class fielder as well, with a really safe pair of hands. I can't remember him ever dropping a catch. These exceptional qualities, combined with controlled aggression, make him a complete cricketer.

Akshdeep Nath

What can I say about Akshdeep Nath? The first thing that comes to mind when I think about Aksh is his appetite. I have never seen such a glutton! If ever there is too much food, call him—he will finish it off.

Aksh is a typical Uttar Pradesh boy who speaks in proper UP slang, but his ways are very different. He has often surprised me with his knowledge. He is well mannered and has a balanced head on his shoulders; you can trust him blindly. He is someone who will keep your secrets, come what may. Even when provoked, he won't have anything bad to say. You can make out from his body language that he is basically a fun-loving person and likes to keep things simple. I have never seen him boasting about anything. He would take a brilliant catch and, when praised for this extraordinary effort, he would simply smile and say, '*Aise hi hath me aa gaya, yaar.*' (It just came into my hands.) He plays with a lot of confidence and has won us many matches. He is probably the best fielder in our side. His never-say-die attitude is infectious to the hilt. His crucial catches and run-outs have immensely contributed to our victories. Aksh has always been a major player. He was rewarded with the status of being the fielding captain of our team.

I know at times he was irritated because we made him bat quite low in the order, but the fact is, we relied on him heavily. We didn't want to lose him early. He was the pillar of our middle order. But he never showed dissent; he always took it in his stride and tried his best to contribute. He is the complete package. His sixes are worth watching as he clears the rope with the slightest of effort.

There is one more aspect of his personality that probably many of you don't know. He writes poems and is very good at it. He is spontaneous about it too. He wrote one for me—it is still there in my diary. His love for poems shows that he is a very sensitive person. He is my crisis man for sure and a great prospect for the future.

Sandeep Sharma

Sandeep Sharma, or Sandy, the Shahenshah of swing bowling, was the spearhead of our bowling attack. This guy can really swing the ball, and by swing I mean 'sswwingg'—it's a double movement. He has mastered the art of inswingers mixing it with the occasional outswinger, thus toying with the batsmen. He has literally fooled batsmen, who have gone on to leave his balls and stood surprised on hearing the sound of the ball hitting timber. The expression on their faces would say it all.

Sandy is a mature lad. He was of great help to the team. Normally, fast bowlers take to a corner of the field after completing their spell, but this guy will find ways to be in the thick of things. His biggest weapon is his deceptive body. He is of medium height, while his chest and shoulders are moderately broad. Often, batsmen facing him expect easy balls.

I can tell you that Sandy has the most athletic of bodies. He can fly with it. He did a few somersaults after we won the quadrangular series in Vizag. And I will never forget the catch he took against England in the quadrangular semi-final in Australia. He was standing at cover point and the batsman had hit the ball very hard in the air. We saw Sandy jumping at least four feet in the air, stretching his right hand and the ball vanishing into his hands! It was probably the best catch ever taken by a fast bowler of his height. Sandy has come to the rescue of our team more often than anybody else. Whenever I found the situation getting out of my hands, he was my first and last resort. His yorkers were bang on target, and then he'd follow them with a slower one right on the spot.

His on-field brilliance runs parallel with his enthusiasm off-field. His sense of humour is unmatchable. He can imitate anyone in the world. He is very good at telling stories and anecdotes, which he shares with us in his own *andaaz*. He can mock anyone. He would keep us glued to our seats with his narrations, while not giving any of us a chance to speak. At times he would go overboard, creating problems, but since we took everything in our stride, things didn't get difficult.

I remember once he took me on squarely. This was when we lost the match against England. He made some comments about me behind my back. As a captain I could not play deaf to such loose talk, so I confronted him. Later we both realized our mistakes and were sorry for having created a scene that needn't have happened. Today I realize that the confrontation we had, brought us even closer. I sincerely hope to see him in the blue jersey soon. He was a great person to have in the team.

Kamal Passi

The first thing that comes to mind when I think of Kamal Passi is our laughter moments. Passi, the favourite of the Aussie crowd, is a phenomenal character. This guy has a special charm about him. I don't know what it is exactly, but there is something about these Punjabi boys. Their sense of humour is first rate. Passi is from Jalandhar, and a complete desi boy. To deal with him, you need to understand him properly. But despite all the fun I have had in his company, I would never want to share my room with Passi. He is always at the centre of a pool of chaos. I can never forget his quirks. He is so simple-minded and friendly that he gets too friendly too quickly with people, which is what gets him into trouble quite often.

Passi always enjoyed how we focused on his desi style of speaking, but at times I told him to be serious about his communication skills. I told him to learn English. He promised me that he would but he never did. I remember in the second league match against Zimbabwe in the World Cup, when he claimed six wickets, rather than being happy he was tense. After claiming his fifth wicket, he came to me and hugged me in his own style. Then he slowly muttered into my ears, *'Yaar, agar Man of the Match mil gaya, toh mere sath tu bhi chaliyo.'* (If I get the Man of the Match, then you should come with me.) He was excited to take six wickets but nervous about speaking at the post-match ceremony. Finally he stuck to his Hindi–Punjabi accent and somehow managed the ceremony. Later on, he realized that he had appeared too nervous and was tense again wondering what everyone would think back home. We tried our best to calm him down but failed. Ultimately, a comment on his Facebook profile calmed his nerves: A female fan wrote, 'Oh Kamal, you looked so cute on TV.'

Passi is someone who is hyperactive, jumping around without any reason, but can be quite moody too. I had to be careful in handling him. We had our differences but as we spent more time together we started respecting each other more. Buddy, please forgive me for all the misunderstandings. I know you are a very simple soul. Just believe in yourself. You have it in you. I have only one thing to worry about when it comes to you—*Bhai, kamara saaf karna seekh le!* (Brother, learn to clean your room.)

Ravikant Singh

Ravikant Singh is a Bengali boy who has made it to many a headline for his lethal spells during the World Cup. He was lucky to find his name in the fifteen-member squad after Mohsin was diagnosed with malaria just a few days before the tournament. He made the most of this opportunity and bowled some decent spells, taking five wickets against Papua New Guinea and giving Australia a tough time in the final.

He doesn't look like a fast bowler—they are usually tall, strong and aggressive. He's thin and of a medium height. When you look at him, you wonder whether he can really bowl quick. But trust me, he was the fastest in our group, very nippy. His ball skids after pitching and his action is as smooth as butter. He relies on pace and off the pitch deviation. He has got a wonderful action. He is surely a bowler to watch out for.

I don't know much about him as he joined us rather late. But I do know that he is not someone to mess around with. Then he will be in your face straight away. Treat him well and he will reciprocate well. Ravikant, you just have to pitch it up and you will be a winner. Keep working on your strength and learn quickly. India needs a bowler like you who can generate good pace and is as accurate as you. *Tum karbo re, Ravikant!* (You will do it.)

Sandipan Das

Sandipan Das, another Bengali boy, whom we call Shondippon, has a West Indian hairstyle, and is soft by nature. A well-mannered and polite boy, he is a talented middle order batsman. He plays without fear and is known for hitting huge sixes. I didn't get to spend much time with him either, as he too was a late inclusion in the side, but from whatever little I saw of him, I could make out that he is a friendly guy. Unfortunately, he didn't get to play in any of the matches and thus couldn't prove his mettle, but he has got all that it takes to be a champion. I would love to have even half of his soft nature because even that is enough for anyone to earn respect from people around. Take good care of yourself, buddy, and keep working hard. Sooner or later, you'll achieve what you are capable of.

Vijay Zol

A seventeen-year-old who looks stronger and more mature than most of the other boys, Vijay Zol has a dense beard on his face and hair on his chest, which always kept people guessing about his age. He has a strong build and an equally strong mind. He is highly talented and way beyond his contemporaries. His domestic statistics say it all. In the last season before the World Cup, he amassed 1700 runs in the Under-19 Cooch Behar Trophy. He scored more than 400 runs in just one innings. This speaks volumes about his class as well as his temperament. This boy is special. He has a solid defence and can also bat with authority, a rare quality. A true Maharashtrian batsman in approach, he values his wicket and doesn't throw it away easily.

I haven't spent much time with him off the field. He used to be with Akhil and Aparajith, his closest buddies. I am sure he is going to dominate domestic attacks, and since he is eligible for the next U-19 World Cup, trust me, he is going to rock it. He will milk the bowlers for sure. Vijay, just keep practising and learning. Work on your fielding. Do more speed work and you will be a complete cricketer. I learned a lot from you, especially the temperament that you demonstrate while batting. I wish to copy it and do justice to my own game.

Akhil Herwaldkar

Akhil Herwaldkar is a sweet boy who has just made a beginning. He is yet to explore the flavours of the world. A quiet and low-profile Mumbaikar, his childishness is his USP. He was the so-called baby of our team. He's only seventeen, and yet he is a good timer and placer of the ball. It's a treat to watch him run with his short, heavy steps. Though he struggled to find a permanent place in the playing XI and remained in and out, he is certainly a class batsman.

He would score 30–40 runs and suddenly when everything seemed all right, would get out. It happened time and again. But it's a matter of time and a little application. I am confident that he will sort it out.

Akhil has his dinner by 8 and sleeps by 9.30 every night. Parties and outings are a big NO. He doesn't mingle much, and stays with his two friends, Zol and Aparajith. He has another U-19 World Cup to prove his mettle. He will be a game changer and a match winner for sure.

Hanuman Vihari

Vihari 'Aadu Aadu', that was the punchline for Hanuman Vihari. Vihari is a big boy but his voice is rather soft. We teased him a lot about it. I rate Vihari very high on my list. He is a good batsman with solid technique. After putting up a good show in Vizag, he was dropped from the next outing for unknown reasons. It was a big shock for all of us, as we had faith in his abilities and were counting on him. I remember sending him a long, consoling message to motivate him during that low phase. He must have worked really hard. There was a sea change in his fitness and batting when I saw him next. But he couldn't make it to the Asia Cup as well. I was sure his dream to play the World Cup had faded. But when there is darkness all around, there is an extraordinary opportunity for light to make its way and make things bright. God opens a new gate, if you deserve it. And such a thing happened to him.

Unfortunately, my best buddy, Manan Vohra, broke his finger just two days before the World Cup journey. And he was replaced by Vihari. Manan was unlucky but Vihari got his due. That's life. Nothing is permanent, so one needs to be patient and keep working hard. Though he couldn't make the most of the opportunities he got in the World Cup, Vihari has been doing a great job in the domestic circuit. He is a frontline batsman for Hyderabad and bats with flair. He is an excellent fielder too. He handles pressure exceptionally well. I like his tough attitude and would like to imbibe some of it in myself too.

Prashant Chopra

Prashant Chopra, or PC as we call him, is an old friend of mine, dating back to the early years of my cricketing journey. We played for the same club, under the same coach. His father is also a coach and I have practised under him at the National Stadium, Delhi. We used to open for our club in the Under-12 tournaments and have also played as rivals in school matches—I played for DPS, Noida, and Prashant played for Sardar Patel Vidyalaya, Delhi. So we have a long connection. And we ended up opening for the U-19 Indian team.

PC was a late inclusion in the side. Having scored big runs for his state Himachal Pradesh, he found a place in the team for the World Cup. He is an opening bat who plays with aggressive flair; he is also a brilliant fielder, a part-time bowler and wicketkeeper. This guy is unpredictable. He bats with an upright stance, likes to play on the up and doesn't mind hitting the ball in the air. No wonder he can decimate any opposition on a good day.

He sinks into complete silence and becomes numb while batting, as if he has taken a *maunvrath* (vow of silence). I love to talk when I bat. He, on the other hand, doesn't utter a single word, leaving me alone to my own company. I used to get bored. But PC, hugely superstitious, would be busy with his own routine, and I would tell him, '*Bhai, kuch bol le, yaar.*' (Brother, please say something.)

Vikas Mishra

'*Mishraji, ab woh fielder nahi raha,*' that's what we used to tell Vikas Mishra about his improved fielding. Mish is very close to me, and has been my Delhi teammate since our Under-16 years. Though you won't see us together that often, we actually know and understand each other very well. Mish has loads of experience behind him. He is probably the most senior player amongst us when it comes to playing at the higher levels of domestic cricket. He debuted for the Delhi Ranji team before me and has played in the Duleep Trophy too. His height is a major advantage to him. With occasional sharp turn, he straight away puts the batsman in doubt. He is unpredictable, which makes him lethal. He is a nice bloke off the field too. He keeps experimenting with his looks—I personally like him in the French beard. He's quite self-obsessed and at times arrogant, praising his own beauty and height, which always makes me laugh. *'Mishraji, bas bhi karo'* (stop it now), I would tell him.

His best friend is his BlackBerry; he is religiously addicted to the BlackBerry Messenger. He is never bored when he's alone. I quite like his habit of reading newspapers daily when he is back from practice.

This book and our journey are incomplete without two more names. Unfortunately, just before the team had to leave for Australia, one of them fell prey to an injury and the other caught malaria. Having spent two years with us and playing all the other three tournaments, they were greatly missed during the World Cup. Their support and best wishes helped us in our triumph. You will both always remain a part of the team, Manan Vohra and Mohsin Sayyed.

Manan Vohra

'*Yaaron ka yaar*', my brother and closest friend Manan Vohra is one of the best guys I have ever met. He has a lion's heart and is a lovely human being. He was my roommate in my NCA days. Not many know this but our association goes back many years. We must have been twelve when we first met at Bedi sir's camp in Dharamsala, followed by Under-16 ZCA and Under-19 camps. Both of us have more or less similar physique and facial features, so most people call us twins. Yes, we are like brothers separated at birth. When we bat together, the scorer has difficulty in identifying who Manan is and who Unmukt. There have been times when people have wanted to meet me and ended up bumping into Manan, taking him for me.

Manan is a very good cricketer. His only problem is that he loves to be depressed. He is always concerned and worried about the future. He needs to enjoy cricket more and worry less about the results. I have had tough times with him trying to console and counsel him. He has a collection of slow, sad songs, and loves listening to them when alone. But when in a good mood, he can be very funny and can make you laugh. I will always remember the time we vacationed together in Kausali (Himachal Pradesh). We laughed our hearts out for two full days. He is someone you get attached to instantly.

As a cricketer, he has played some good knocks for Punjab in age-group tourneys. He was with us for all the three U-19 tournaments we played before the World Cup. Unfortunately, just before our departure to Australia, he fractured his right thumb in a practice match. I can't begin to imagine the pain and disbelief he must have felt for missing the World Cup. That was really sad. But I am sure there must be something else in store for him. God is very kind. He will compensate for it.

I missed him terribly. The tour and the win would have been different in his presence. But it was not to be. We can't fight with fate. He is a superstar, and small hurdles can't stop him from achieving the heights he is destined for.

Mohsin Sayyed

The typical fast bowler from Maharashtra, Mohsin Sayyed is a bright lad. He is quick and just seventeen. He is also eligible for the next U-19 World Cup. I am sure he is going to stun many a batsman with his speed. All our U-19 batsmen had a tough time facing him in the nets. I first saw him during the U-16 Hanumant Singh Trophy. I was playing for North Zone and he was representing West Zone. He was fast even then. I remember his spell in the quadrangular series in Australia when the batsmen struggled to put bat on to his deliveries. His bouncers come fast and skid through, while his yorkers are toe breakers. He is a left-arm bowler, which makes his angle even more difficult, especially for a right-hand bat. I am sure he will get more lethal in the coming years.

By nature, he is quiet and reserved. I have always seen him sporting a smile. Even after getting dropped from the side due to ill health, he didn't show any disappointment. He took it in his stride and faced the difficult period with a big smile.

Bharat Arun

'Unmuktchen': that's what Bharat Arun sir likes to call me, in a Chinese accent. He is someone with a big heart, the best coach I have played under. He is the coolest possible dude (although he is in his fifties) and enjoys life to the fullest. He is a great motivator and a friend to every member of the team. I have never seen him behaving harshly. He is a great family man, and a classy cook to boot. And he still possesses the naughty elements of a teenager. For the things that he has done and said to me, I would have to write another book. A Good Samaritan, if ever there's one.

The best thing about Arun sir is his understanding of the mindset of each player. Even if I were batting terribly he would never go into the technical aspect of it; he preferred to work on my mind (keeping in view the context of the competition). He would come to me and say, 'Buddy, you are the best Under-19 player in the world. You know it, I know it and everyone knows it. You don't need to worry about anything, man. Others need to worry. Just take your time, and you are mature enough to turn the tables single-handedly.'

He would give me so much confidence that I used to feel elated. All my doubts would fade away. Trust me, in my Under-19 career I felt like a king. I was always high on confidence. I knew I was the best and that's what helped me perform at crucial junctures. This feeling of being the best didn't come automatically, it came because my guardians (the support staff) helped me in realizing that. Arun sir constantly reminded me of my abilities, and his trust in me has made me a stronger personality. Arun sir demanded 100 per cent on the ground; off the field, he didn't care.

He was always sceptical about the hours I spent in the nets. He used to come running and tell me to stop. In fact, he made sure that I didn't bat on certain days. He used to insist that I take a day off—he always wanted me to enjoy my game and life. Too much cricket is not good, he would tell me. He puts a lot of emphasis on loving and enjoying life.

He would call all of us to his room and chit-chat. He ensured that the atmosphere always remained light and sporty. We would sit for hours together in his room and laugh our hearts out. At times, the hotel staff would come up and request us to keep our voices low. But there was no stopping us. His Hindi with its slightly Punjabi accent was in itself enough to get us rolling on the floor holding our stomachs in breathless laughter. Those were memorable moments.

Arun sir is also a master chef; his culinary skills are amazing. All said, he has taught me the real meaning of life; he's taught me that life has to be enjoyed and there has to be a balance between work and leisure.

He made this journey so beautiful for us. *Tussi great ho,* Arun paaji.

R. Sridhar

You can compare Sridhar sir to Alex Ferguson. He is a rock star. He has this special ability in 'man management', which is as important as anything else, especially in a team game like cricket. He's been the best guide and motivator I have ever met. He pumps you up so nicely, carefully choosing his words and hitting the bull's eye. Then all your doubts disappear and you just start looking at the target, nothing else.

Officially, Sri sir was our fielding coach, but that was only in designation. He not only worked with us during our fielding sessions but also took care of everything else, from throw-downs to inspecting the nets, always giving us very useful feedback. His words of wisdom have influenced me a great deal. Even now after the World Cup, I am in constant touch with him. He motivates me whenever I am down. I call him up before big matches for a final word and he is right there delivering the perfect line which gets me going. He is a great human being, always ready to go the extra mile. His favourite line, *you always have more time than you think you have,* has worked wonders for me. Whenever I am under pressure, on or off the field, I take a few deep breaths, say this line to myself and there I go, feeling much more confident and in control of myself.

It's really important to be aware of what works for you because there cannot be just one way to success. Sri sir has given me so many options to choose from, making it much easier to find out what works for me. You need people like him to encourage you, to push your limits and discover who you are and what you are capable of. I lay so much emphasis on this because at my age it's really difficult for anyone to have a full understanding of himself and his game. You always look to someone senior who is knowledgeable enough to realize your potential and guide you. We may be blessed with eyesight, but may not have a vision. And Sri sir was the one who gave us that vision, creating opportunities for us to do justice to our potential.

I am always amazed when I speak to him because every time you speak to him, you learn something. He has always got motivating tips or inspiring real-life stories and anecdotes that keep you glued to him. He was always available for the players. At any time, he would be surrounded by a group of curious boys.

Sri sir has this habit of experimenting with his looks. He is a regular on Facebook and Twitter, and keeps posting fresh photos. None of us could believe he was more than forty years old—he looks so young and fit. He was the first one to bring an SLR camera on tour and many of us duly bought one later for ourselves. He has such good taste in photography. I am sure most of the pictures of the boys in action on the field, flaunted on their respective Facebook profiles, are taken by Sri sir.

I imbibed so much from Sri sir that at times I start behaving like him, giving lectures to fellow players, trying to set a goal for them, trying to boost their morale . . . That's not a bad sign.

Sudarshan V.P.

Everyone calls Sudarshan V.P., 'Sud'. I call him Chetta, which means elder brother in Malayalam. At first glance, this guy doesn't look like an Indian; he has more of a South African look to him. When he speaks, mostly in English, he has a foreign accent, which confirms your guess. In my first two years at NCA, before his official appointment as trainer with the Under-19 boys, I hadn't ever spoken to him. He has something of the air of a martinet about him— you don't want to mess with him. He keeps his distance, loves his own company, and is punctual. He doesn't open up too early, talks very little and focuses on work. But if you spend some time with him and build a good rapport, he is great company, both on and off the field. He is an unusual person, but somehow our wavelengths matched to perfection, which has brought us close to each other over the years. Obviously, we have spent most of our time together in the gym. He is a hard taskmaster and pushes you to the limit, which is the quality of a good trainer.

He is forty-two but is stronger than all of us. He can lift some really heavy weights. He is particular about the gym and very committed to the diet aspect as well. He made sure every one of us had a balanced, nutritious diet and were drinking enough water. He made us stop drinking soft drinks during the competition phase, because these aerated drinks dehydrate your body. He always focused on us getting enough rest. In all, he made us a more disciplined unit, which helped us tremendously on the field.

We share a great relationship. Chetta always tells me that I am a man for the big occasions. When the chips are down, he bucks me up to get ready to deliver when it matters the most, and fortunately it has almost always worked. I look forward to working even more with him. I really want to become as strong as him so that I can smack the ball out of the park using my core muscles.

Sanju Singh

Sanju sir is a helpful and generous person. He was like the mother of our family, a gentle, caring person. You always found him smiling. He is a straightforward person and doesn't hold anything back. But at the same time, he avoids giving you direct solutions. He will twist and turn and make you think hard and finally extract the answer from yourself.

Sanju sir was our video analyst. He recorded our batting and bowling videos, and helped us significantly by making us aware of the intricacies of our techniques. The job of a video analyst is never easy. During matches, he sits the whole day with his laptop, recording each and every ball. A video analyst is supposed to be active throughout the whole match, 600 balls in total, plus the extra balls bowled.

He has been of great help to us in figuring out the key strengths and weaknesses of other teams. I remember how, during the quadrangular series in Australia and also the World Cup, we would sit in front of the laptop and keenly watch the videos of opposition teams. The bowlers would look at the opposition's main batsmen, their scoring areas and difficulty zones, and make a plan likewise; similarly, all our batsmen would look at the bowling attacks and the usual tendencies of our rival bowlers.

More than a video analyst, Sanju sir is a keen observer of the game. He himself has played a lot of cricket. He would never say anything during team meetings, no matter how much we asked him to, but would put his views forth to any individual who walked up to him. He is a simple soul and has always supported us with all his heart.

I have spent hours with him chatting about various things. I like his simplicity. He is someone who gets excited quickly. He has big goals. He was really disappointed when India lost to Pakistan in the quarter-final of the 2010 U-19 World Cup. I am really happy that we could bring a smile to his face by winning. I remember his last lap from the dressing room to the pitch when we won the Cup. That hug from him was special.

I don't know why he still says 'thank you' to me every time we meet. Of course, as always, he won't explain anything directly, but I understand what he means and I would just like to say that it's I who should be thanking him for all the love and support he has given me over the years. Thanks, dada, for giving us such a family atmosphere and always making us feel at home.

P.R. Srinivas Rao

The role of a physiotherapist has evolved over the years and now it has become quite important because it is not only limited to ensuring a quick recovery from injury but also involves proper guidance on how to prevent injuries and stay fit and healthy; this includes following a proper diet, drinking enough fluids and taking enough rest. A physio also ensures that all your muscles are activated and each muscle is doing what it is supposed to do, and not take support from some other muscle. In short, a physiotherapist makes sure that even the smaller muscles are working in tandem with the bigger muscles of the body, because, most of the time we forget that smaller muscles are also important, and we just focus on the bigger ones. The physio works with you on a proper pre-rehabilitation session to make the brain aware of the minor muscles and their movements, thus preparing you to stay away from injuries. Post-injury, he works with you on rehab sessions to get the movements in sync and strengthen the injured part of the body so that it doesn't break down again.

P.R. Srinivas Rao sir was our physio, and with all his experience, he understood the importance of a disciplined diet and gym workout. He would constantly goad us, while at the same time remain friendly.

Srinivas sir is the one who deserves credit for the team's awareness on fitness. He made sure that none of us struggled at the camp, even though at times we were negligent and lost in having fun. We would sit together and gossip with Srinivas sir. Passi and Sandy used to tease him a lot, making life difficult for him at times. We enjoyed ourselves a lot in his company, though he preferred to be by himself. We even overcame his reluctance and made him dance quite a few times. His broken Hindi was also a source of amusement. We always had fun with him.

We used to call him 'Cheeni Chacha'. Cheeni Chacha kept a low profile. One thing that really surprised us was his addiction to Maggi noodles. He lived on Maggi through the whole Aussie tour. When I think of Srinivas sir, I also think of pain. He would give us circular massages with his elbow which was meant to eventually ease the pain, but it used to hurt a lot when he was actually giving it to us. In such situations, the initial pain is a sign that the body is healthy. His hands had a magical effect, and the pain would soon fade away. His contribution was crucial to our triumph. Srinivas sir, you are too good a man!

Vinod Phadke

The thought of a manager accompanying the team for tours has always troubled me. A manager is appointed by the BCCI and is usually seen as the 'board's person', who is appointed at the last moment. He's not part of the team during camps but accompanies it during tours, taking care of the finances, lodging, tickets, clothing, etc. After the tour, he submits a report to the BCCI on the team's performance and behaviour. So, one is always conscious of the manager's presence. But the way Vinod Phadke sir handled the job changed my entire perception about the manager's role.

Vinod sir was our manager for the quadrangular series in Australia. He's Goan and we thought he would be laid-back, but when we first met him we were all struck by his seriousness. But first impressions are not always right. As time went by, he turned out to be a generous and kind-hearted man who did anything he could to help us out. He was such great company.

He, in fact, gave us the liberty to enjoy and never stopped us from anything. Instead, he became a party to it. He ensured that everybody had fun and didn't let the pressure take a toll on us. He would even organize barbecue meals for us at the beach, at his own expense. Those exciting and light evenings are memorable. Vinod sir, tusi great ho!

Though we lost the first three matches consecutively in the series in Australia, he never put any pressure on us, nor did he interfere in team meetings. He, in fact, announced a surprise bonus of 50 dollars for a bowler taking three wickets or a batsman scoring 50 runs, and 100 dollars for five wickets or a century. We were pleasantly surprised. These small incentives sometimes make a huge difference, especially when you are young. These incentives excited us and our relationship with him strengthened. Though he must be in his fifties, his enthusiasm for life is boundless. He is uber cool. We had so much fun with him on the first tour that we desperately needed him for the World Cup. We had a team high on self-belief, mutual trust and respect, a caring support staff and a manager like Vinod sir. The unit was formidable. So was the result.

9

Lessons from the Masters

The only person who is educated is the one who has learned how to learn and change.

—Carl Rogers

I've always vouched for the importance of interactions—with seniors, professionals from other fields, one's mates. Interactions help you understand varied points of view; it helps in finding solutions to problems. It takes you into the life of another person; it shows you a way that is not your own, one that is away from your own old, beaten track. This gets even better if you are in communication with the masters of your field. A nineteen-year-old couldn't ask for a greater reward. It's always a dream-come-true to be able to speak to the greats of the game, people who've carried the burden of an entire nation on their shoulders for a long time, the saviours of cricket. I've grown up watching them, idolized them and dreamt of emulating their feats. And here I was, face to face with them, in the early days of the U-19 team.

Diary Entry

MEETING RAHUL DRAVID

U-19 World Cup preparatory camp, NCA, Bangalore
23 July 2012

Today, we had an interaction with the legend Rahul Dravid. What a human being! Wow! You feel so relieved and at ease when you meet a man of his status and calibre. He is a true cricketer. I formed this opinion from the forty-five minutes we chatted with him. He started off by telling us about simply being aware of ourselves. He told us that all great players he has played with were very aware of themselves. Awareness of self is really important, not only for cricket but for all the departments of life. You should be aware of yourself, your personality, your strengths, your weaknesses, how you react to a particular situation, things that upset you or charge you up, what suits you best, and so on. Cricketing awareness is important, but self-awareness is even more important. We should be always analysing ourselves. He told us that as we grow, we would have to deal with different pressures in different phases of our life, but if we know ourselves and our surroundings well, we can face those situations better. Every individual has a different routine, and a different way of looking at the same problem. You just need to be aware of your routine. It is not that tough. Sticking to what suits you is the best way to approach any problem in life. He emphasized on practising with a purposeful intent and goal. If we have taken up cricket as our career, he said, then we should be focusing on just cricket. It's always good to avoid distractions as they interfere with the normal processes of your mind.

I wanted to probe his mind and take some valuable advice, so I asked him a couple of questions. I asked him how he prepared himself for the big matches. He told us that no match is big or small. All matches should be played with the same intent and determination. Secondly, he told me that he used to take four vows before going into any match. They were:

1) Physical: He used to make sure that he has trained enough, and he is feeling good about his body and there are no niggles.
2) Mental: He is well prepared for the match, and has assessed the pitch and the opposition bowlers as to how they are going to bowl at him.
3) Technical: This is to do with whether he was getting into good positions while batting, the balance, etc. He used to make sure that he had done a couple of net sessions a day before going into a match.
4) Emotional: This was in making sure that he was in a good space mentally. He used to settle all his emotional issues well before a match, whether they were related to family or girlfriend, or whether they came from within him.

After ticking off these boxes, he would feel nice and confident of himself. If one has prepared well, obviously the confidence automatically grows.

He also talked about the importance at our age of understanding the game without worrying about the results. Winning the World Cup doesn't guarantee that we will play for India. Someone may play in a year, someone else might take five years, while others may never play for India at all. So the whole focus should be on improving one's game, learning as much as possible and understanding oneself. He gave us the apt example of a Chinese bamboo. Unlike most other plants, Chinese bamboo is unique. When this bamboo is planted, watered, and nurtured for the whole growing season, it does not outwardly develop even by an inch. Then, in the next growing season, the farmer continues to irrigate, fertilize and care for the bamboo tree, and yet nothing happens—it fails to grow just the same. As the seasons go in and out, the farmer continues to care for the bamboo for four consecutive years. What could really be discouraging is that the farmer has nothing substantial to demonstrate for all of his labour in caring for and cultivating the plant. Four lonely years of hard work and caring, and yet you have nothing!

And then, in the fifth year, you must be prepared for something so amazing and incredible!

All the hard work pays off in the fifth year because that Chinese bamboo tree, at last, grows, and not just normally like other plants. The bamboo tree shoots up to more than eighty feet in just one season. It's not that it has not been growing for five years; it has been actually growing from the inside. That is the time it has taken to spread its roots over a large area and make a solid base. Once it has established itself completely, it takes only six months to shoot up, that too to a height of eighty feet. A great lesson in patience, persistence and hard work can be learned from the story of planting the Chinese bamboo.

A similar lesson could be applied to us too. As young cricketers, we too could grow in the same way. It doesn't matter whether the results come quickly or not. What matters is that we are focused on the game, learning every day, honing our skills, and being patient with ourselves. Time is an important factor. Our processes should be correct; then the results will come automatically. Rahul Dravid said that our age was the right time for us to work on our game, understand the intricacies of batting and bowling, and to spread the roots as deep and wide as we can.

It was a good lesson, in fact a reminder not to run after success, but after perfection, and to practise with precision. Success will automatically follow. It was really nice and enlightening to interact with such a kind and noble person. Dravid is someone who is really attached to his roots. This interaction will definitely help our team immensely.

In the same room as Sachin Tendulkar

Before we left for Australia for the U-19 World Cup, the BCCI arranged a very special meeting for us. We went to Mumbai to meet Sachin Tendulkar. I was, of course, over the moon, and wrote it up in my diary:

Finally the D-Day, 3rd August 2012, has come. Tonight, we are leaving for Australia via Dubai. It will be a nineteen-hour flight. I don't know how we are going to make it. But at the moment we are not worried about that. We are all excited and thrilled. It's a great honour for us to represent India at such an important event. Many people came to see us off. There were flocks of media people outside our hotel to catch a glimpse of the players and get a word from them. I was as busy as everybody else in the team attending calls from friends, relatives and the press.

We left Bangalore in the afternoon for Mumbai first as the flight was supposed to leave from Mumbai that very night. The board had scheduled our departure so that we could have some time in Mumbai, and had arranged an interaction for the team with the god of cricket, Sachin Tendulkar. Sachin agreed to meet us; he, of all people, would understand how important it is for us to have self-belief, and meeting him would contribute to that. It was indeed a great privilege for us to be able to interact with the living god of cricket. We were excited to meet him. We had been discussing about this moment and waiting for it from the second we heard about the meeting. Cricket is just like a religion in India and Sachin is definitely a god. We had all seen him play since our childhood, and we adored him. Sachin is my all-time hero. All the players in the world are on one side and Sachin alone on the other. No adjectives are enough to describe his talent and devotion to the game. He seems to know everything.

I was slightly apprehensive about meeting him, but once the discussion started, I tried to get as much as I could from it. Sachin was practising at the Mumbai Cricket Association,

Bandra Kurla Complex. We were supposed to meet him there. We reached BKC where we were greeted by many BCCI officials, including Sandeep Patil sir and Lalchand Rajput sir. BKC is a lovely complex. We were taken to a meeting room on the third floor. Everything was nicely arranged over there. Five minutes later, Sachin entered and what a moment it was! I was seeing him up close for the first time in my life. Though I had played against him the previous year in the IPL, I didn't get to see him so close. He is actually quite short, though tall in his deeds and achievements. The thought ran through my mind that here was a man who has dominated bowlers all over the world. But he did not look like that big a man. His hands appeared thinner than mine. Looking at his height and body frame, I concluded that physical appearance has got nothing to do with mental abilities.

Sachin started off by making us more comfortable. He called us closer and told us to be as interactive as possible. He told us about his experiences as a cricketer, how he grew up practising for hours correcting his technique, the importance of staying in the present, and so on. I asked him how he has dealt with the tremendous pressure over the years. He said that pressure can only affect you when you feel you are pressurized. You cannot avoid pressure but you just say to yourself that it is something normal and natural. The best thing to do is to control your breathing and stay in the present. Pressure comes when you are either thinking of the past or the future. He cited a few examples when he was in such situations and how he handled them. He further elaborated that it is very important for the team to stay together. That's the ideal way to feel better and less pressurized. Enjoying each other's company can really help one stay calm.

He also talked about being in the zone. It is basically switching over to your subconscious mind. That is the ideal state of mind to be in while batting. He told us that whenever he was under pressure, he would get into that subconscious state and he ended up playing really well. I found his answer very true because I have also experienced my subconscious mind taking over. But then I have also heard people saying that all these top players know what is going to happen the next ball. So they plan their shots. I asked Sachin about this and he said that this does happen, but that doesn't mean they don't get out when they plan. He has himself got out like that many times, but getting out or not is not the point of the exercise—you need to look at the probability of success. If I think that my chances of being successful are higher than the chances of failing, then I do take the risk. He told us of an incident when India was playing against Australia. He was batting on 90. Mark Waugh was bowling, and had a straight deepish midwicket. So Sachin took a few couples placing the ball square in that area. This forced Mark to move that fielder squarish. But then Sachin targeted the midwicket gap. I believe this mastery comes with experience.

Sachin also told us of the importance of picking up singles. He told us about a Ranji game he was playing against Tamil Nadu, when Mumbai was chasing a mammoth target of 485 runs. He scored a hundred in that match. Mumbai needed 42 runs with two wickets left. Sachin was batting with Abhay

Kuruvilla. Mahesh was bowling. All the fielders were placed on the boundary for Sachin. Mahesh used to bowl a slower one by jumping from close to the umpire. Sachin had understood that signal. So the next time Mahesh bowled him a slower one he stepped out of the crease and hit the ball out of the park. He used to push for two runs here and there so that the fielders came under a bit of pressure. And then, when the fielders came in fifteen to twenty yards, he used to hit it over them.

He recounted a few nice anecdotes. It was a great feeling to chat with him. He has that aura that attracts people to him quickly. I asked him many questions—I just did not want this opportunity of a lifetime to be wasted. As soon as we were done, we gathered around him for a photo session.

Talking to Sachin was a great learning experience. It only increased my desire to bat with him in the middle for India. I don't know if this dream will come true ever. The interaction was followed by a press conference at BKC. By now I had become used to such press conferences. The same questions are repeated every time. My uncle, sister and grandmother had also come to see me by then. They got a first-hand look at my interaction with the media. I took all of them to my hotel room. My sister Samragyi met all my friends. It was a hectic day, and in the evening we left for the airport.

V.V.S. Laxman

Though we didn't get a chance to interact with V.V.S. Laxman in a group, I was lucky enough to speak to him at the NCA a couple of times. I've never seen a more down-to-earth person. The 'crisis man' of the Indian team is a gentle, soft individual. He loves to interact with the youngsters and is always smiling. He has congratulated me on all my feats and it feels nice to see that he follows my performances so eagerly. His kind words of wisdom have always moved me. Though he himself is used to getting a lot of praise, he never shies away from praising others. I've had a few chats with him on cricket. He has shown a keen interest and has tried to help me to the best of his abilities. I remember an instance, while at the NCA, when he made it a point to come to me from another part of the gym to wish me luck for my upcoming tournament. I was mesmerized. I have loads of respect for you, sir. Thanks for everything.

10

The Campaign Kicks Off

He who knows the way leads the way all the way.

—Sir Vivian Richards

Diary Entry

REACHING AUSTRALIA

6 August 2012

It was a really chilly morning in Brisbane, and we had to drag ourselves out of bed early because of our scheduled early breakfast and practice. The cold was intense. You don't experience such cold in Delhi where visibility becomes low and the fog takes over. In Australia it's a bright, clear cold—no fog, and the sun shines. It makes you want to go out in the cold. The people there don't mind the cold either. They are all wearing half-sleeved shirts and shorts.

Shivering as the cold wind stabbed me I entered the coffee shop half asleep. The Australians are a sports-loving people. There was a huge screen in the shop showing the Olympic Games. Coincidentally, it was showing the most awaited event of the Olympics—the 100 metres men's race featuring the world's fastest man, Usain Bolt. The race really set the tone for us. Suddenly, we got out of our morning drowsiness. Bolt won it easily. He appeared by far the best of the lot. The way he took the lead midway was just amazing. He got ahead of the herd in no time and clocked 9.62 seconds. Good lord! How can anyone run so fast! Jamaicans are amazing people; their crazy dance moves and love for music are incomparable. They live life to the fullest. I can also say this because I had a great time with Andre Russell, a Jamaican player in the Delhi Daredevils team. A real character, his energy level is unmatchable. You just cannot stop him. He is always charged up.

After witnessing Bolt's historic win, we pushed off for the practice session. Brisbane is a lovely city. In fact, all of Australia is beautiful. It always feels so nice to look through the window at the landscape. Sometimes it seems unreal, as if you are looking at a painting.

We reached the practice area in half an hour. There was light moisture on the ground because of the cold weather. I did some knocking before going in to the nets. Initially, my feet were not moving. But I batted well in the nets. I wanted to bat more so I went into the other net for throw-downs. I wanted to try out some pull shots, but was unable to get the timing right. I started getting frustrated. I do not know why I am getting so easily irritated these days. Then

Arun sir came to me and discussed a few things. I was being too hard on myself, he said. Indeed, I wanted to attain perfection, and when I couldn't, I didn't feel good. That's where I needed to improve. Every batsman has a few grey areas, but they cannot forget the good 98 per cent of their batting because of the bad 2 per cent. I have a tendency towards comparing overmuch. When I see someone play a really good flick shot, I feel like mastering that shot myself too, and if I am not successful I get frustrated. Arun sir told me to always rely on my strengths and not chase perfection every time—that I would get there automatically with practice. He even tried to boost my confidence by saying that I was probably the world's best batsman in that age group, so I needed to feel good and not worry about what I did not have. It was a nice lesson to learn, but easier listened than done.

After practice we went back to the hotel to change our clothes and then hurried to the stadium for a few photos in match jerseys. The shoot was accompanied by a lecture on anti-doping and anti-corruption. Both these areas are really crucial in today's time. A player needs to be very vigilant. You may become a victim without even knowing. It was an interesting session.

After the lectures the teams left, except for the captains, coaches and managers, who stayed behind for the opening ceremony. A few big names like David Boon and Michael Kasprowicz were also present. David Boon was the match referee for the tournament. There were long and boring lectures on playing conditions, rules, behaviour, etc. I was feeling too drowsy in the conference room and so were others. I could see a few bored faces in the room. And then it was time to pose with the World Cup trophy with all the captains. For a second I looked at that trophy earnestly. I knew I had to fight a battle to own that trophy. All this was followed by a dance programme, which concluded the inauguration ceremony. I had imagined a big ceremony like that in the Olympics and at the IPL, but then I had forgotten that it was an U-19 tournament.

Practice matches

We started off on a high note. Having won both the practice matches, our spirits were high in the dressing room. Everyone was charged up. Everyone had gotten into the groove. A perfect ten in the warm-up matches! We could only hope we carried the same momentum into the coming matches and scored a perfect ten every time we entered the field. I knew we were capable of that. We played the first practice match against Sri Lanka. All the fifteen players got a chance to play. Trying to push ourselves, we decided to bat on a new turf. I was batting well and feeling really good. But a bad umpiring decision sent me back to the dressing room. Such a thing usually happens to me—I am generally not lucky in practice matches. I get dismissed in weird ways. But that is part of this game. And I also don't want to get lucky in these matches. I know that when the big match comes, god takes my side. Let all these weird things happen in practice matches alone.

We didn't do well as a batting unit. We could only manage 191 runs. But the good thing to happen was Hanuman Vihari's return. He came back to the side with a bang. He batted really well and scored a 50. With his return, the middle order became quite stabilized. Now I could open the innings. Our original plan had been to have me at no. 3 in order to have a long batting line-up, but now there was no need of that; with Hanuman there I could rely on my middle order. The total of 191 was very much gettable. But our bowlers did a fantastic job by restricting the Lankans to 160. Everyone chipped in with a few crucial overs. Passi, especially, was superb. He hit the correct line and length, something he used to lack before. Fielding, as always, was good. I bowled four overs, and although I didn't get a wicket, I was economical. I was also giving air to the ball and pitching it in the right areas. We won the match without any difficulty.

The second match was against Afghanistan. We batted first. I got off to a flier. I was hitting the ball at my own sweet will. I scored 70 off 50 balls. The team management sent me a message that I had batted enough and it was time for me to retire in order to give someone else a chance to get a feel of the conditions. I did not want to let go of the opportunity, so I started scoring fast, and soon got out trying to hit a six. As the match went on, I left the ground to buy some stuff from a sports shop. While leaving NCA, Yuvraj had asked me to get him socks from Australia, because one doesn't get thick cotton ones in India. Also, some of us wanted the Aero P1 thigh guard. So, with the money that I had collected, I bought a few of them. It was a batting paradise and the fast bowlers had a tough time. Harmeet dominated our bowling. He took five wickets. He was back in form and turning the ball very well. Due credit should be given to the Afghani batsmen for reaching close to the target. They batted really well. It was good to see such nice talent emerging from such a small country. I wish them luck for the future.

Later in the evening, we decided to go out partying. I got hold of Jason Inglis, the local manager, and asked him to take us to some of the happening places in Brisbane. It was our last night in Brisbane and I wanted to make the best of it. Harry and Passi, my party pals, came along with me. We had dinner at a nice rooftop restaurant. Wednesdays in Brisbane are normally very quiet. All the pubs and discos are nearly empty. But Fridays and Saturdays rock. Disappointed, we hired a taxi, but to our good fortune, the cabbie turned out to be an Indian. He took us to a place that would be rocking that night. It was a 'uni night'. Amazing! The crowd was really good and the music was awesome. University students are always on a high. These guys dance out of their skins; they are really expressive and bold in their dance moves. They always leave me wondering if I can ever dance like them. I wonder how they go deep into themselves and forget their surroundings. Whenever I go to discos, I always come out convinced that I should join a dance institute and learn hip hop and salsa. I don't know when I will have the time to do that but I really want to learn dance and also play the guitar.

Diary Entry
11 August 2012

TOWNSVILLE

What a lovely morning! Beautiful sunshine. Townville is a beautiful town in north Queensland. It can't get better than this. I mean, here I am, sitting in the open balcony of my hotel room, basking in the sun and writing my diary and watching the inaugural match between Australia and England. I just woke up and switched on my television and there it was, live stuff happening on the ground. Now I am feeling much better; initially, I was feeling a bit nervous. That's natural before a big tournament. Especially when you know that the matches are going to be telecast live and billions of people will be watching it. I could visualize myself going for the toss tomorrow with the great Wasim Akram doing the pitch report, and being interviewed by Sanjay Manjrekar. Oops, my heart is beating fast again.

There is good news today! There was a selection committee meeting yesterday for the India A tour to New Zealand. I have made it to India A! I will have to join the India A camp as soon as I am back from the World Cup. It's good for me that I have come one step closer to accomplishing my dream of playing for India. This has really added to my confidence. Inclusion in the India A side will definitely help me stay more motivated and focused in the matches to come. I am quite happy but I'm trying not to get too excited. I don't want to distract myself from the task at hand—the World Cup. I will talk about India A selection only after I am back home with that coveted World Cup trophy. Till then, it's only about giving the best here.

So the much-awaited start of the tournament is here. Tomorrow is our first league match against West Indies. When I close my eyes and think about the journey, it seems that it has just started. Just a short while ago we didn't know each other. I didn't talk to some of these guys and they didn't like me. Whenever I think of any member of the side, the only image of the person is the one in the NCA. We spent so much time together at the NCA that now we know each other inside out. We never noticed how we have become a well-knit unit, one big family. I don't know why I keep emphasizing this family thing, but I really do feel it in my heart. Family doesn't mean that we don't fight or argue with each other. It means that whatever we do, we are all in it together. That is an invisible and unbreakable bond. I will always cherish this bond.

The West Indies side is unpredictable. One thing I can be sure of is the fact that they have good fast bowlers. Their spinners won't be that good. Craig Braithwhite has already been playing for the senior West Indies side. He is the one to look out for. Obviously, we can't take them lightly. They are tough but so are we. We are prepared and ready to roll. We have discussed some of the key factors. I spoke to the boys about my experience as a young lad in the IPL. This is the first time most of them will be playing in such a big event that would be telecast live. So the pressure is obvious. I should ensure my boys are not feeling the tension. I spoke to each one of them to steady their nerves. I told them to follow the same things they have been doing over the past matches and do nothing different—don't think of it as a big event. Doing different things can affect your psyche. I told them that staying together and supporting each other and, most importantly, enjoying each other's company can help to minimize the pressure generated by the big matches.

Now I am all set. I just want to put all the feedback we have got over the years into action. It's time for execution; time to deliver.

Diary Entry
India vs West Indies
12 August 2012

Oops! We lost the first match. Well, not to worry. I don't know why I am chilled out even after losing the match! There is no sign of disappointment in the dressing room. All the players seem to be OK with the loss and we believe that we will definitely win the remaining five games. Well, that's a healthy sign too. If you look at past tournaments, we have stumbled initially but recovered very soon and gone on to win the trophy. The moment I came off the field Arun sir said it's really unrealistic to expect to win eight matches in a row, including the warm-up games. That shows the kind of belief and confidence we have in each other.

Just a brief reflection on what went wrong. First off all, it was a bad toss to lose. We were put in to bat. It was a treacherous pitch for batting. The West Indies bowlers were quick, while the seaming nature of the pitch made things more difficult. And it was not just the seaming; the pitch had a few cracks, and once the ball landed there it could go either way. The ridges on the pitch also made it worse as a the ball would rise sharply or keep low once hitting them. I had a tough time in the middle. However, I stuck there till the 20th over but never felt that I was set. All credit goes to their bowling. We could do nothing. Nevertheless, I think we showed great temperament. I don't think any other team would have lasted as long as we did. I also had trouble sighting the ball, as did the others. The sight screen is quite small at the Tony Ireland Stadium. All the West Indian bowlers were really tall and their release points were much higher than the sight screen. So there was nothing behind them that could help us in sighting the ball. I was just reacting on instinct.

We managed to get 166. Sandeep bowled really well. Rush was a disappointment. He could not generate pace and was bowling too slow. Harmeet bowled well. His loop on the ball made it really difficult for their batsmen. Vikas was average, and could have bowled better considering his experience. Overall, however, our bowling unit did a great job. We stretched them to the 47th over. Needless to say, earlier, Smit had played a brilliant knock under pressure. His batting average must have increased as it was rather low earlier. We used to tease him about his low average. Rush had a better average than him. Jokes apart, Smit did well under pressure. I hope he continues with the same form and doesn't get excited like he usually does. We will definitely come back stronger and fiercer in the coming matches.

It was also our first match with live TV coverage. I have played matches that were telecast live before, but as a team we are not used to it. There was no pressure but when I spoke to the commentator, Danny Morrison, after the toss, I stumbled a bit and repeated a few words. Like 'I guess'. I am used to giving interviews to media but this was something new. Instantly answering to things that you don't know much about or are unsure about is difficult. I was slightly embarrassed after that and upset too. It was playing on my mind. I spoke to Sri sir, and he assured me that by the end of the World Cup, I would be perfect at it. The post-match interview with Sanjay Manjrekar went off much better. But there's a huge scope for improvement. Obviously, it will take time; I should not worry about this. I remember a similar thing had happened in my first press interview. We also discussed the TV commentary, and how the commentators were discussing our batting and bowling. Ian Chappell was saying about Smit Patel, 'Can Patel shut his mouth and concentrate on his keeping?' This was after he had given a bye. We made lots of fun of Smit over this, but in good taste. All told, it was a good experience and now we will go on and win the rest of our matches!

Diary Entry
India vs Zimbabwe
14 August 2012

It seems like I have come out of a nightmare safely. Zimbabwe gave us a real tough fight. We were lucky enough to take a hold over the match at the right time; otherwise, as some of the players thought during the match, we would have been out of the main contest and relegated to playing the Plate matches of the World Cup. Well, I was confident about victory but the way Malcolm Lake was batting, it seemed that it was his day and nothing could stop him. This bloke was hitting the ball at will and clearing the field with ease. Sandy went for quite a few runs, followed by Vikas in the next over. It really made me think. I was a bit confused about who I should give the ball to. Truth be told, I had also started chanting mantras and praying to my isht dev (family god). Then Sandy put together his act, ably assisted by Aparajith and Ravikant. They bowled really well. Ravikant was debuting for India. But he showed no signs of nervousness and was very accurate in his line and length. He also bowled a few yorkers at the death. But the star of today's match was none other than the biggest entertainer in the team, Kamal Passi.

Passi hit a purple patch today. As people say, on your day whatever you touch turns to gold. Passi was the man today. To begin with, he went into bat in the last over. He played five balls and scored 24 runs! He was trying to hit the ball straight and it would go soaring over the fine leg fielder for a six. He hit two sixes like that. I mean two sixes with the edge of the bat is crazy. He hit one over the midwicket boundary as well.

Before he had gone in to bat, Passi, our local manager Jason, and I were chatting, and I cracked a joke on Passi's body structure and his inability to hit sixes. Passi, as always, was boastful of his ability to clear the boundary and, as expected, he reminded me of the matches where he had hit a six. I responded cheekily, 'Really?!' But today after he hit those sixes, I thought I am never going to hear the end of these three sixes! The cherry on top was of course that such hitting was taking place in a match that was being telecast live. So as he was coming out of the ground after his innings, we were shouting, 'Passi, now smile, you are being watched on TV.' And he raised his bat. It was going to be his day. He bagged four wickets in his first spell, followed by two in his last. He was also involved in a run-out. Actually, when the chips were down and I was about to give the ball to Vikas, I realized that it was Passi's day. He had that lucky wand in his hand today. So I tossed the ball to him. It was a do-or-die situation. But as I expected, he did his magic. A bang-on yorker followed by a slower delivery and that was it; he had crafted a way out for us. It was a dream spell for Passi, that too in a World cup match. I was really happy for him. The figures of six for 23 is awesome for any bowler.

Funnily, when Passi scalped his fifth victim, instead of getting excited, he got nervous at the prospect of speaking in English at the Man of the Match presentation. He even came to me for a crash course in English. Finally, he somehow managed! We laughed ourselves silly during the presentation.

I scored 78 in the match, missing out on a big one. I just threw my wicket away. Well, I hope to do well in our next match against Papua New Guinea. Prashant also batted well. He scored a brisk 50. But our middle order could not capitalize on the good start that we had given them. With eight wickets in hand, we scored just 110 runs off the last 20 overs. That was poor. We need to work this out. The only reason for this poor performance was the fear factor. We need to play fearless cricket to succeed. The biggest problem I feel is a lack of communication in the middle between our batsmen and their lack of awareness of the match situation. Our batsmen in the middle have not been talking to each other about the state of the game and what they need to do. We have been emphasizing a lot on the fact that we should play out the full 50 overs. And that our batsmen should control the urge to hit every ball. Take it to the 47th or 48th over, was the mantra. But our batsmen have been getting restless far too early and in the process, getting out.

It's now high time to convert our learning into application. The next match should be easy but we should not be complacent. We should practise hard to see ourselves in the play-offs.

Diary Entry
India vs Papua New Guinea
16 August 2012

I am not in the best mood to write but I will try to push myself. It's very late. Today was a bad day at work. At times, things don't go according to plan—they might turn out the exact opposite to your expectations. That's what happened today at the Endeavour Park. It was our third and last league match, against Papua New Guinea. I don't know much about this country but I certainly knew that it was a newbie to cricket and they wouldn't be a threat to us. We could use this match as practice for the coming games. The batsmen really needed some confidence and this was a good chance for all of us who were not amongst the runs to score and gain some confidence. That was the only reason I was adamant about batting first on winning the toss. Arun sir was in favour of bowling as were all others, but I was firm in my decision to bat first. As I saw it, there was no point in getting them out for a small total and then us scoring those runs quickly. If we could not overcome Papua New Guinea, then there was no point in thinking that we deserved the World Cup. If we wanted to be champions, then we have to think like champions, rather than play it safe.

Perhaps I was wrong to take such a chance at an event as prestigious as the World Cup. But batting first was my idea and perhaps I was overconfident. It was an opportunity for me as well as others to score big. Playing with weaker sides alters your thinking. Rather than thinking about the process, you start thinking about the result. You are not thinking of 30s and 40s, but 100s. You don't look for singles and twos;

you are aiming for fours and sixes. Thus, you get far, far ahead of yourself. You stop thinking about the team. As a batsman, you don't want to react; you want to act. Everything vanishes; your routines change; instead of playing the ball by its merit, you want to hit hard. You don't want to defeat them—you want to thrash them. No matter how much you tell yourself to respect the opponent and stay focused like you would in the big matches, it's really difficult to get in that zone. I had found that I was fighting with myself in both the previous matches. I wanted to hit out from the very first ball but I had stopped and reminded myself that I had enough time. I really don't know why I take more pressure in such matches.

So I won the toss and elected to bat. The very first ball I faced, I hit for a boundary; the next ball I tried to punch off the back foot again, but got an edge and it carried to the slip fielder. I was in deep shock. It felt as if I was in a bad dream. The fact that I had got out in the very second over, made me lose my mind. Instead of blaming myself, I started criticizing the ICC for including such a weak team. I was shell-shocked. I had missed making a biggie. Getting out is bad enough, but it's even more disheartening to see the other batsmen thrashing the bowlers. When a bowler sends out nice, flighted, juicy full tosses, trust me, it's painful to watch what you've missed out on. Runs that could've been in your kitty are going into someone else's account. I tried to divert my mind because I could do nothing except sulk in the dressing room and clap at the sight of my share going to the others. I may sound like a selfish jerk, but honestly speaking, you can go to any batsman and ask him whether I am wrong or right in carrying such an attitude. Spending those three and a half hours on the bench is a tough task when you get out so cheaply against a weaker team.

But that's how life is. Cricket is a cruel game. What you expect doesn't happen; and it happens when you don't expect it. It hurt me very badly as I was not ready for such a situation. But it also made me realize some things, and I tried to keep them with me. At times I have forgotten the mistakes I've made—well, not forgotten exactly, more like I have buried them in my subconscious. It's important to recollect and analyse the mistakes that one makes. With so much of cricket happening, you tend to forget your mistakes, but the more you keep them with yourself and learn from them, the better it is for you.

The match on the whole was diametrically opposite to what we had expected. We were 100 for five at one stage. I don't know what had happened to our batsmen. Aparajith was unlucky. He got run out. But the rest of the batsmen just threw it away. Vihari played a bad shot; Prashant was playing well on 58 before getting out casually; Aksh played a loose shot to get out. I am worried about Aksh. He is the strength of our middle order. But it has been a while since he has scored runs. He is definitely under pressure and low on confidence. It is showing. Previously, when he walked in to bat he looked liked a king, a finisher. He would counter-attack if the chips were down. He is a match-winner and capable of taking us home from any situation. I need to talk to him and make him realize his worth. I have been talking to him a lot about his excess aggression on the field. By excess aggression, I mean overexcitement. He is an overconfident guy. We tried to calm him down a couple of times. But I think it's better to have an overexcited guy in the team than a timid one. I want him on the front foot and not on the back foot. I am sure he will make it when it matters the most.

Smit is another one who's getting out repeatedly making the same old mistake. Hundreds of times we have talked in our team discussions about staying at the wicket and playing till the end. The idea was that at least at two batsmen, including Smit, should bat on till the 45th over, so that we could exploit the last overs to the hilt. But in this match, we accelerated far too early and got out. We tried to accelerate after the second power play and left the last 10 overs for our bowlers to go and bat. This batting power play hasn't turned out well for us till now. A batsman's presence in the death overs can get us more runs than the presence of tail-enders. Smit and Zol had a good partnership of 70. Both were going great guns. This was our last batting pair. Then suddenly, Smit swung wildly to the only good bowler Papua New Guinea had, and that too when the fielder he was trying to clear was right at the fence. Three wickets fell in quick succession and finally we could manage only 205 runs against Papua New Guinea on a pitch that was a batting paradise. Smit got a long ticking off from Arun sir. He was really angry at Smit's attitude. Zol had played a good and useful knock of 72.

I know that our batsmen are struggling a bit but this is not the time to criticize them. I spoke to Arun sir as well and both of us agreed that we were in a spot and that there was nothing we could do at the moment except give the boys loads of confidence and try to bring out the best in them. I spoke to my teammates and told them to rediscover the hidden spark they possess. We have come a long way and tough times are a part of the journey. But I have faith that soon we'll find out a way. The best thing about this team is that we peak at the right time. Hope we can pull it off again. I am also due for a big score. As for the match, ultimately we won it, but they gave us a good scare.

On Monday, we will be playing the quarter-final against Pakistan at Tony Ireland Stadium. It's going to be an exciting battle between the arch rivals. We still remember our loss to them by one run in the Asia Cup quarter-final and the tied match in the final of the same tournament. Now by the law of averages, it's our turn to turn the tables against them and I am confident of that. We are going to make history. We still have three days to go. So it is time to go around and have some adventure. We decided to go to the Magnetic Island. I wanted to go there last time during the quadrangular series but had missed it.

I like adventure. I have this habit of exploring new places. Many a time, when my teammates were not ready to come with me, I have gone with my support staff to explore new places and restaurants. I don't like sitting idle in hotel rooms. I have already gone bungee jumping and someday I will do a free fall too. I am a buccaneer. Only Sridhar sir, Kamal, Vikas and I were ready to explore the island; the rest decided to stay at the hotel. Somehow I was not happy with their decision as it was a wonderful opportunity for all of us to go out and have a great time. I too don't mind late-night parties once in a while, but I am always ready to venture out the next morning instead of sleeping. OK, boys! It's my life. Magnetic Island is eight kilometres off the coast of Townsville. This fifty-two square-kilometre mountainous island in Cleveland Bay is a suburb of Townsville. The island is accessible from Townsville Breakwater to Nelly Bay Harbour by ferry. There is a large twenty-seven square-kilometre national park and bird sanctuary, and you can also walk to a number of tourist destinations such as the World War II forts. Those of us who went had a wonderful time. As for those who didn't, I feel sorry for these young guys who prefer to rest rather than explore such wonderful places. But I know guys like Akhil and Aparajith are very particular about their routine. They go to bed by nine religiously. But then, they miss out on all the fun.

Diary Entry
Quarter-final: India vs Pakistan
20 August 2012

What a match! It cannot get better than this. The match between the arch rivals lived up to expectations, and had one of the closest finishes we have ever seen. History did not repeat itself this time—we snatched victory from them. (Pakistan had won the quarter-final against India in the last U-19 World Cup in 2010.)

It was a good toss to lose. Pakistan won it and elected to bat first. I was surprised at their decision. Fielding first gave us a boost and then Sandy started off brilliantly by taking two wickets in his very first over, giving us a kick-start. Getting such a start really inspired us and we showed great energy and athleticism on the field. There was a lot of cheering and all of us were on top of them. Some great display of bowling by Sandy and Passi, and 10 overs on the trot by Ravikant made things a lot easier. This guy Ravikant is turning out to be a great revelation. He is bowling superbly and accurately. He bowled those 10 deadly overs and demolished their batting. He was always on the money. Though he took only three wickets, he bowled as if each of his balls would fetch a wicket. Our bowling unit was at its best. Harmeet also chipped in with oodles of spin and drift, making the batsmen's lives miserable. We were also getting ample crowd support to keep our adrenaline flowing. They were singing patriotic songs and cheering loudly. It was amazing. We got them out for 136. Restricting Pakistan to that meagre a score was a great achievement. The boys were really happy and the atmosphere in the dressing room was charged with the belief that we were going to win easily.

But things changed when we went to bat. Pakistan returned fire with fire. I was the first one to go, trying to hit a wide ball over the point boundary; it went straight to the third man fielder who caught it brilliantly. I was done. I was feeling so pathetic at that moment. I don't know why I was not able to concentrate today. My mindset seemed to have changed. I had tried to do something different. Instead of seeing off the new ball, I wanted to hit it hard. I wasn't able to control myself. This usually doesn't happen but it happened today. I was really disappointed. Also the fact that unlike in the previous tournaments, I have not been able to make runs so far in this World Cup is weighing on my conscience. I am used to getting runs for my team and staying in the thick of things. This time it has been different so far. I would not have forgiven myself if we had lost the match. It took everything we had to reach that target of 136. Our batsmen just didn't want to stay at the wicket. It was two-way traffic, one was coming in and the other going out. Two quick wickets after my dismissal set the tone for Pakistan. We were on the back foot again. Aparajith and Zol had a good partnership till Zol (always a candidate for run-outs) ran himself out. And then Aparajith, Smit, Passi and Ravikant followed.

The last pair was at the crease and we still needed 12 runs for that now-distant victory. Harry and Sandy were batting. It seemed the match had slipped away from us. Twelve runs seemed like 120 runs. Our hearts were beating furiously. I was literally trembling from the pressure and excitement. I made all sorts of promises to god: 'Please, god, we don't want to lose this match to Pakistan. I swear I will never make such a mistake again in my life.' I was trembling and chanting shlokas. Meanwhile, Sandy was just defending the balls in front of his pad. Harry was playing fine but you never know what might come to his mind. He could do anything.

It then came to this: two runs required; the last over on, with all the Pakistani fielders in single-saving positions. Harry hits it hard over the infield. The next second we were all over the place. The long faces turned into gleeful ones. We all ran onto the ground and jumped on Harry, and there was a wild celebration. I must say that both Harry and Sandy had played very sensibly. I give them the credit for taking us to the semi-final.

Aparajith got the Man of the Match award for his knock of 51 runs, one wicket and four catches. He played really well today.

So the law of averages worked as I had thought it would. I just cannot explain what I was going through towards the end of the match. My dream of winning the World Cup was on the brink of being shattered. A huge thanks to the prayers of so many back home, who were glued to the screen.

We are playing the semi-final against New Zealand on the 23rd and I am desperate to score big and do well for the team. I am thankful to my teammates who have brought us to this stage; now it is my turn to do something and present them the World Cup.

I reached for my BlackBerry and updated my BBM status: 'I can feel d cup in my hands.'

Diary Entry
21 August 2012

Why is there so much time between matches? I am sulking in my room, cursing and criticizing myself for yesterday. I am getting desperate now. I want to go and bat and score piles of runs. It's the World Cup and I have made no big contribution. That's getting on my nerves now. Deep inside, I keep telling myself that whatever is happening is for my larger good—I cannot be the cynosure of all eyes every time. There are other guys in the team who should also enjoy the fun of becoming a hero. You sometimes need to make up the rear. No one is bigger than the game. I need to respect that.

But I am going crazy at the moment. I have never been so desperate for a match till now. I want it. I want the cup in my hands. I want to win it. I am just visualizing myself scoring those big tons in the semi-final and final, and taking the cup home.

To make it worse I find myself getting angry and irritated with comments back home. I don't want to destroy my confidence by listening to repeated discussions of my performances. Now I am consumed by the hunger to score runs and I am challenging myself. I could watch TV, but as of now I don't want to get distracted by what is happening in India. This is a pressure situation and I need to learn to handle it. You just cannot run away from it, especially as captain.

Diary Entry
Semi-final: India vs News Zealand
23 August 2012

And we have reached the final of the World Cup!!! What a feeling! No words can express my feelings. Let them remain locked inside. They should erupt only after I hold the coveted cup in my hands and kiss it. I am so happy for everyone in the team. This was our collective dream and it is now just a match away. I can see it coming to me. As if it was made for me.

Today I realized that individual milestones pale in comparison to the feeling that accompanies a team's success. This team started its journey two years ago and that journey is now nearing its end. Obviously, some of us play together for our states, but most of us may never again play together as a team. Earlier, there were small groups in the team, but with the passing of time, our togetherness and unity has increased. The bond between us has become stronger and stronger, and it feels really good when some teammates come to you and pat your back, telling you that they are with you: 'We will back you. Just go for it. You are the best.' I really cherish the friendship we have developed in the past two years. It's amazing.

Just one more match. Just one more day of good cricket. Obviously, we are all here to play good cricket, but right now everything is focused on the team and the tournament. I am not thinking of anything else. I just want to do well and get the best out of my boys on Sunday, when we take on Australia. It will be the first time India would be winning the World Cup outside Asia. The previous two were won in Sri Lanka and Malaysia. Wow, that will be a fantastic achievement.

There is a lot of buzz back home too. I heard that my house was crowded with media people doing interviews of my parents and live shows. My parents are also having a good time. Friends, relatives and everyone who know us are flooding us with good wishes. These media people sometimes go crazy. They made my parents garland each other. (It was my father's birthday today. I found out later that the cake I had ordered for him online had just reached home the moment we had won the match, and that too in the presence of the huge media contingent. What a moment for them! What a gift for my father on his birthday!)

I hope my parents get used to this. I am also loving it. The best part is that we are outside India, so we are away from all that hype. That has really helped us to solely concentrate on our cricket.

Now to the match report. I lost the toss again and we were put into bat as is standard practice here. We got off to a good start. Both Prashant and I controlled the game nicely. The ball was moving quite a bit. But that is expected in these conditions. We forged a 50-run partnership. But suddenly I lost my concentration and missed the line of a slow medium pacer and was bowled. I had done all the initial hard work. I should have capitalized on that good start. Prashant and Aparajith carried the game forward. Prashant got out after scoring another 50. He should not be throwing away his wicket like this. Our middle order stumbled a bit. We should have scored around 250 but we could manage only 209. But it was not a bad score in these conditions. Our bowling has been our strength. I knew that if my bowlers bowl to their potential, then we could take the match away from the Kiwis. And we were bang on target. All the bowlers have had great spells in this World Cup. Fortunately, all of them have clicked. Harmeet is bowling at his best at the moment. I have never seen him giving those loops and revolutions so perfectly. And so is Ravikant. He has proved his mettle. Our fielding, too, has been top-notch throughout the tournament.

Aksh has done us proud by his athleticism on the field. He is a live wire. In the bowling department, Passi has come good. He is swinging the ball really well and also generating good pace. Sandeep is at his best. No words for this guy. Though he hasn't taken many wickets, he is the leader of the gang. His experience is immense and all my fear goes away when the ball is in his hands. He bowls yorkers at will. Hitting against Sandy in the death overs is never easy.

The Kiwis had a good fourth wicket partnership. But we believed in ourselves and kept pushing ourselves. We knew it was just a matter of one wicket. There was great enthusiasm on the field. Aksh took two brilliant catches. The communication was superb between us. Everything went according to plan. A change in bowling worked for me. Finally, we won the match by 10 runs.

I loved the post-match presentation and interviews. I praised my team for its effort.

Now the big Sunday awaits us . . .

11

The Triumph

*I believe in an athlete's life, winning is important, but,
the journey is more meaningful! The constant pursuit towards
overcoming one's own limitations and always challenging
the part of you that says you will not or cannot win! I am
convinced that everybody has, at some time in their life, faced an
equivalent. Something that feels insurmountable.
My, perhaps unsolicited, advice is enjoy the ride! Let's face it,
roller coasters are far more thrilling than merry-go-rounds!*

—Abhinav Bindra

Diary Entry
Final: India vs Australia
26 August 2012

Are we done? Is it really over? Is this what happens when you
win a tournament like the World Cup? Oh, yeah! We have
won the Under-19 World Cup. I am still not able to fathom

what it means to me and the team. It has not sunk in. I thought I would go bonkers, run in the streets, tear my clothes, and do all the crazy things people do on winning such a cup. But I am very normal at the moment. Fully conscious of my being. I had promised that I would try my hand on some drinks today, though I am a teetotaller, but I could not take more than a sip.

But I was enjoying watching the others enjoy themselves. We went to an Indian restaurant to celebrate the evening. It's very difficult to explain the feelings and excitement floating around us. It could not have got better than this. This is the ultimate. We have now nothing left to prove or achieve. I have played the innings of my life, and I am overjoyed that it happened on such an important occasion— the World Cup final!

A few hours have gone by since that magical moment, when the winning shot came from Smit's bat and the team went berserk running into the ground. I am still not able to absorb it. People are constantly calling me and congratulating me on our feat. They are trying to tell me that I have become a hero. My teammates hug me whenever I pass by. They, too, are trying to tell me that they are actually relishing my heroics. I can't deal with too much praise. I get embarrassed. But today, people are just praising me. I am flattered. I know it's a big moment in our lives. We have all been dreaming about this day for the past two years and finally we have achieved it.

To be completely honest, I am very relieved. I'm feeling very calm and mentally relaxed right now. There are no more matches, no more meetings and strategy breaks and no more pressure of performing and winning. The mission is finally over and it's time to enjoy ourselves before the start of a new mission. The feeling is sinking in. Soon, it will be back to normal. I am not overexcited. I want to just keep this as a memory and move ahead. But I do not think it is possible. The support staff and the whole team are over the moon right now and they are going to pull me also there.

When I went in to bat today, I was fresh and probably in the so-called zone. I had faith and belief that we could chase down the target of 225. Though I knew we would have to bust our guts to reach that target, I did not betray my emotion to others. A few heads were down when we came back to the dressing room after the first innings. Our bowling was good. But the Aussie captain Will Bosisto batted brilliantly to get them to a respectable total. After four early wickets the Aussies had some good partnerships. The pitch was really nice to bat on. 225 seemed a hell of a score. Our batting unit had had a tough time all through the tournament. Pakistan had already given us a nightmare. We had struggled badly to score 137 against them. So the chips were down and I could see a few worn-out faces.

Before getting into the ground to bat, I followed my routine and felt really fresh. It was quite unfortunate for Prashant to get a legside edge to the keeper. But I had a good partnership with Aparajith. We kept the scoreboard ticking. At one stage, it all seemed very easy. Aparajith is a gem of a player. His elegance and smoothness is unmatchable. His free-flowing batting gave me confidence. Everything was going according to plan. But then, Aparajith got out and we were struggling again. Vihari and Zol followed

Aparajith to the dressing room in quick succession. We were now 97 for 4 and suddenly I could feel the pressure building.

I cannot explain how, in such a tense situation, I could remain so relaxed and calm, in control of myself; at other times, I feel totally out of place, unable to control myself. I had struggled to control myself against Pakistan—I knew I should play safe initially, but then had lost control and got out playing in the air. But today was different. It was as if everything had slowed down. There was a big crowd at the Tony Ireland Stadium today. But I was so engrossed in myself that I barely noticed the crowd or heard its shouting. I was concentrating thoroughly. I also did not look at my score even once. I knew looking at the scoreboard could invite trouble—it has happened to me in the past. Yes, your score creates pressure. It disturbs your mind. You start thinking and planning your personal milestones. I was just keeping an eye on the overs bowled, the runs required and the number of overs bowled by each bowler. That's it. I talked to Smit a lot and kept boosting his confidence. I told him that we have done it in the past and we could do it again. He was not that confident early on, but I never let him feel insecure. I told him to believe in himself, have faith in me and we would take our team through. And man, he did the job.

While batting out there, I was really thinking a lot about when to accelerate, when to decelerate, which bowler to attack, etc. I think communication is the key to building a partnership. The more you communicate, the more you are aware of the situation. It helps you in strange ways. For example, when I was telling Smit almost after every ball what he is supposed to do, I was indirectly keeping myself aware of the situation. I became more active and responsible. I told Smit to play his natural game and trust his abilities. I said all those things that I hoped would boost his self-belief. I kept reminding him that he should not play any premeditated shots, that I trusted his batting ability. I reminded him of earlier instances when we had successfully chased down similar scores in a similar situation. I told him to just react to the ball and then everything would fall into place automatically. It was great that he trusted me and followed the instructions willingly. Undoubtedly, he played a great role in today's victory. He did not get distracted by the lanky, big-mouthed Aussies.

It was around the 34th over when I realized that we were struggling to cope with the required run rate. But I knew the pitch was really flat. If we had wickets in hand, we could make a charge any time later and neutralize the pressure of the increasing required run rate. It was really important to stretch the game and get closer to the target. At times I had this urge to go for big shots, but I stopped myself. I remembered Dhoni speaking during one of his post-match conferences about the importance of taking the score closer. He had said, 'During the 38th over, a bowler would not be under that amount of pressure as he would be in the death overs. So it's better to take him on later rather than taking chances so early.'

When Smit joined me, I was thinking of somehow reaching a score of about 125. I had planned to start the countdown after that, because that was the time when the pressure would start affecting the Aussies too. I had been a fielding captain in such situations and I knew that it was only a matter of one good partnership and the pressure would fall back on the bowling side. 100 runs is nothing if you have wickets in hand. I was quite relieved when we crossed 125 without losing any more wickets.

Today my heartbeat was in control and had slowed down, and I never felt any pressure. I was chanting a few mantras; yes, I was tense when three wickets fell in quick succession. There were also the thoughts drifting into my mind that this was the World Cup final and we had to win it. I was also thinking about what might be happening back home. But then I chanted the Gayatri Mantra and was focused again. I did not want to think about anything that would distract me from that moment. These mantras can have a great impact on your mind. Chanting 'Om' really helped me maintain my calmness and took my breathing to normal. I get relaxed and more focused while batting when I chant 'Om' before the bowler delivers the ball. I take a short breath in and exhale in synchronization with the shot I play. It helps me channel more force into my strokes. I don't know how it was all happening automatically today. I hit six sixes—all of them from the middle of the bat and straight in the V (midwicket to cover). I was hitting the ball really well. Controlling one's breathing has a vital role to play in batting (as also in all other activities). I know it is not that easy but I will definitely try to recollect those feelings every time I go in to bat. I was also aware of the fact that the Aussies had four main bowlers and all of them had almost finished their quota of overs; so, they would have to bowl their irregular bowlers, which meant that it was important for me to wait for them. We could take chances against these bowlers and that's what we did. The planning was bang on and we pulled off an amazing victory.

I didn't even know when I reached my 50. I did not even realize that I had reached my 100. I was so focused today. Only the crowd's cheering and Smit's congratulatory remarks made me realize that I had got to my 100. I had planned before the match that I would pump my fists in the air and show the bat in a particular way if I got a century today, but I did nothing of that sort. I was so immersed in my batting. My whole focus was to get to that figure of 226. I hit a six to complete my century, but that was not deliberate. I did not celebrate much because all I wanted to do was achieve the victory.

I have never been so determined before. The game plan was clear in my mind—I am still in that state of mind. I am feeling like I have just come out of the ground for a short while and I have to go back in again. I remember every single thing that I did while batting. There was one thing I rectified while batting today. We needed 49 runs off 42 balls. I took calculated risks and was adamant on finishing the match before taking it to the last two or three overs. I still feel bad when I remember the Asia Cup final. I had taken the team so close to victory but had got out in the last over and the match had been tied. I feel I dragged it too late, maybe because in that match we did not have many wickets left and I was more focused on not getting out. I was not going to repeat the mistake in the World Cup final. I was more confident this time around. I knew that I could clear the field. I could see the ball really well and was loving putting bat onto ball. Two to three good overs brought us closer to the target. And Smit hit the winning runs, and even though I did a lot of 'huuu haaaaa!!!', deep inside I was feeling very normal. I didn't know why. It felt as if this was just another match. I thanked god for giving me the courage and peace of mind on the day it mattered the most. I was lucky as well—I was dropped twice. But that's the part of the game.

I feel sorry for the Aussies, especially for my friend Bosisto, the Aussie skipper. He had played a mature innings but could not take his team through. I wonder what these Aussies think of me. I have been responsible for both their defeats in the finals (the quadrangular series and now the World Cup). Bosisto met me later that night saying that he had dropped the cup when he dropped me. It looked like I was the only one responsible for their World Cup loss. But that is how it is. God has been really kind to choose me as the man for the final, giving me the strength to make it happen. Yesterday I had been thinking about my performances so far. Just one half-century against Zimbabwe. The tournament had not gone well for me. My average was pretty low. I was telling god that I have had three successful tournaments so far, but why have I not been delivering in the ultimate tournament of my life? Also the fact that I had never played any of my best innings in televised matches was a big let-down. But today, everything changed. I have played an innings that I will remember throughout my life.

People around me are telling me that this innings will change my life. But I know one innings cannot do much. I have to perform continuously and consistently. Until yesterday, my mind was diverted towards thoughts of what would happen if we won the World Cup, how much money we would get, the kind of gifts we would receive, that we would be famous, and so on. But today, I feel nothing. I aspire to nothing. I want nothing. I have the cup in my hands.

There was a big celebration back home. The media has made us heroes. We have become youth icons of our country. At my home in Delhi, there was a huge crowd and lots of media personnel. My mom and dad were being interviewed by everyone. They were surrounded by friends and neighbours. Our housing society had made special arrangements to watch the final on a big screen in the basement. It was two in the morning in Australia and I could not speak with my parents that day. They were also busy handling the media and other guests. I spoke to my friend Utsav, who had gone to my house the night before the match. He told me how people had gone crazy, and also warned me it would be very difficult for me to now step out of my house as I had become a star and people were going to pounce over me for photos and autographs. I felt happy about all this. I couldn't wait to go back to India and see all this happening around. There are around 300 missed calls and over 200 messages on my mobile. I have put my phone aside on the silent mode.

Here in Australia we do not at all realize what we have done because there's not much media coverage and that sort of stuff happening here. But we knew that in India, people had gone berserk. Yuvraj Singh called me up after the match and congratulated me. We had been getting congratulatory messages from all the big shots. Dhoni and Virat praised me and congratulated us. Sachin also sent us a message; the prime minister of India, too, wished us! I even got a tweet from Amitabh Bachchan and Abhinav Bindra. Sunil Shetty and Suresh Raina also called. Everyone had been following us and we had been getting a lot of coverage. The BCCI had announced a reward of Rs 20 lakh to each player. Kamal Passi is really happy that he will buy a car and finally he will get his room done. He has been talking of building a room for himself for the last two years. Finally he would do it. I hope he does not spend this money on unwanted things. Passi has been the crowd's favourite and he was the most excited guy today.

All told, I am quite relieved. It has been a tough tournament. We faltered initially, then picked up momentum and peaked when it counted. That's the quality of world champions. Adversity and tough situations have brought the best out of us. We have had no one-sided victories in the World Cup. Though we beat Papua New Guinea by over 100 runs, they were looking dominant at one point. Zimbabwe gave us a real scare; the quarter-final against Pakistan was a thriller of a match—our hearts almost stopped—and the semi-final against the Kiwis was also a tough one; we pulled it off only in the last over and won by just 10 runs. The final, of course, was the best of all. 97 for 4 and still more than 100 runs required. And we did it. We could not have asked for more.

For me, the preparations started yesterday when I went to visit an Indian family in Townsville at night to pray and take the blessings of god. There was no temple in Townsville.

So all the Indian people assemble at Rama auntie's place and worship there. I really wanted to connect to god. So I called up Shashank, my friend in Townsville and asked him to take me to a temple. I do not know what pushed me to go to the temple at night, but it is rightly said that god himself calls you to his doors sometimes and that's exactly what had happened with me. Maybe I had not been praying as much as I should have, so he wanted me to do that before giving me the strength to perform. That's divinity. The best thing is that as soon as I sat in the mandir, I got into a meditative state straight away. I could connect to god in just a second. I never believed that until yesterday when I actually went there and felt the difference. Trust me, when I meditated in my room every morning, I was finding it really difficult to get into the zone. My mind had been wavering and wandering a lot, thinking of various things. I had also been struggling with my sleep due to anxiety. But in Rama auntie's mandir, the aura of the divine presence was so powerful that I forgot everything about the big final the next day. The vibes were so strong. There were Bhimsen Joshi's bhajans playing in the background and I loved them. I sat there with my eyes closed for around fifteen minutes and actually did not want to get up. I have never felt so peaceful and calm ever before. My heartbeats also calmed down and all anxiety went away.

This is the reason why people go to places like Shirdi, Amarnath and Vaishno Devi to pray to god. It is said that god is within everyone. But sometimes due to bad habits or routines or busy schedules, you forget god or it is difficult to communicate with him. At such times, one should find the time to go to such places or even to a temple, gurdwara, mosque or church; you really find peace there. I have experienced this myself.

After leaving the temple, I was in my best state of mind. I slept really well. I got up the next morning and the first thing I did was upload the bhajans into my laptop. I felt at peace and could feel the vibes spreading around my room. It was amazing. I had got the vibhuti from the temple last night. I gave it to everyone. Now, all of us had god's power. It helped me gain in confidence. I had told Arun sir before the semi-final match that I would lose the toss but win it in the final, and that's what happened. I was very confident of winning the World Cup even if Aussies had scored 300 runs. I had thought of writing a book after winning the World Cup, and I had started writing it three months before the tournament started. Imagine, what would have happened if we had lost that match. But I never allowed my mind to nurse such thoughts. Somehow I knew god had chosen me to complete the task. As Steve Jobs, the co-founder of Apple, stated in one of his lectures, 'You can't connect the dots looking forward; you can only connect them looking backwards. So you have to trust that the dots will somehow connect in your future. You have to trust in something—your gut, destiny, life, karma, whatever. This approach has never let me down, and it has made all the difference in my life.'

When I heard his speech, I could straight away connect to it because that sort of a thing always happens with me. I can't speak for others, but it really works for me. I know many other things about the future as well, though I will not reveal them right now. This is not an empty boast; it is just a prescient feeling and simply an extension of this dictum: the way you think is the way you feel.

The belief was so strong in all fifteen of us and our support staff that it was nearly impossible to lose the cup. We could not even think of such a disaster in the wildest of our nightmares. Just like Shahrukh Khan's character says in one of his movies, '*Jis cheez ko tum dil se paana chahte ho, sari kaynat use tum se milane main jut jaati hai . . .*' (If you want something from the core of your heart, then the whole universe starts working to provide that thing to you.)

On our first day at the NCA, we were boys with tense faces dreaming of being a part of this team, and today we are a proper team who have finally achieved the ultimate dream of an U-19 cricketer: we've played four tournaments and have won all four of them. The U-19 journey is over for most of us. Scoring a ton in my last U-19 match and winning the World Cup is overwhelming. But your journey never ends. The U-19 journey is over only to start a new one. Now we jump into the men's world. Let's hope we rule there too! U-19 was a jump-start but we can't rest on these laurels. It is good to be a part of the history of cricket, but cricketing memory is very short. I hope and wish many of us will play for the country soon. It has been a great batch. A dream team. Our unity, belief, esprit de corps, has been top-notch. You do not need the best guys to win a team game, but you need strong belief, a central focus, and calm heads.

All of us were soaked in revelry. Outside the restaurant we danced to some bhangra beats. There was loud music and dhols. A few Indian families close to us also joined us. I wanted to be a rock star in the celebration, but I found that I was not very excited about it. I felt a deep calmness within. Yes, I was happy and relieved but I had not gone mad about it. I sat at one corner of the bar sipping lemonade, and watched the boys celebrate. It was the best of feelings. I hadn't seen the boys so happy ever before. Giving them a reason to celebrate made me feel on top of the world. I could finally experience what tears of joy actually meant. I couldn't have asked god for more. All those long-awaited dreams coming true. Winning made me more humble. That's what happened with me. I joined my teammates just for a while trying to shake my body, but could not enjoy it much. I was slightly disappointed as not much preparation had been made for the boys to celebrate. We had heard that the BCCI would be booking a yacht for a night party. We had heard so much about the celebrations when Virat's team won the World Cup four years ago. So we expected better preparations. But still, we were happy with our own ways of celebration. I knew the real celebrations would take place back home.

The celebrations began as soon as we landed in Mumbai. We could hear the drumbeats even before stepping out of the Mumbai airport. You all know what happened next. We were literally taken aback. There was such a crowd at Mumbai airport. Media guys climbing over each other to take our pictures. Cops all around. Unknown people coming to us to shake our hands. The amazing expressions on their faces. To be truthful, I had not imagined this. None of us had. The way I was welcomed at Delhi airport and then taken to my home in an open cart, down the same road I had trodden since my childhood but now with a red carpet and well-decorated apartment premises, carving our way through thousands of people, including neighbours and relatives, waving at me, oh, now it feels like a dream, but I know it actually happened. We had actually won the World Cup!

I hope someday I will again write a book, narrating my experience of winning the world cup for all of you. Obviously, that will not be the Under-19 World Cup.

12

My Mentors

When I look back I find that there have been many people who have been there to help and guide me. There are the ones who had a direct impact on my game as they gave me valuable tips to improve it and there are others who taught me how I could transform into a better person. I have gained plenty from the people around me. If I start writing their names out, it will run into a few hundreds at least—from my nursery teachers to cricket coaches, neighbours to relatives, friends to teammates, senior players to support staff, and so on. I have found so many helping hands on my way, so many good people with good wishes for me. It's not possible for me to quantify their contributions.

However, there are four people without whom I would have had no hope of becoming anything in life, forget about playing cricket and succeeding. It is their sacrifice, the amount of time they have invested in me and the vision they had for my future, their planning, their effort and their belief in me that has pushed me so far. Writing about them makes me a bit emotional as I become nostalgic and their contributions take a visual form in my mind. There I was, a five-year-old boy, just like any other kid in any other house, and there they were, my parents and my uncle; as if they had found the ultimate treasure of life, they got hold of me, a clean slate then and began writing the script with their blood and sweat. They abandoned their own goals, aspirations and priorities, and adopted mine. And then there is my coach, Sanjay Bhardwaj sir. His belief in me is so strong that sometimes I think I believe in that belief more than I believe in myself—how can such an unwavering belief be wrong? The most reassuring thing about him is his success mantra: there is no alternative to hard work.

As I write about these four people, I must once again say that I am indebted to many others too, as they too have played very important roles in shaping my game and personality. But the limitations of this book mean that I must be very selective.

My mother, Rajeshwari Chand

When I was nine, both my parents used to work—my mother has since quit (three years ago). They were both teachers. They would leave the house early, at about seven in the morning and come back by 3.30 in the afternoon. I used to go for swimming class at 5.30 in the morning. My mother used to get up very early to make breakfast for the three of us. It would be a proper full breakfast: parathas, subzi, omelettes, oats and milk. Of course, at the time I saw this as a cruel form of punishment, but now I realize how important it was. And then mom would make lunch so that when I came home from school in the afternoon, when my parents were still at work, I would have food waiting. Till this day, she makes an extra effort to be sure I am properly fed.

Mothers and food go together. But for me, she has always been much more than that. Honesty, discipline and punctuality were the most important traits she wanted to see in me. She was very strict about timing. She always ensured that I woke up on time, was regular with my routine, and kept a check on my playing schedule. Eight to 10 p.m. used to be strictly study hours, come what may, every day, whether I had exams or not.

My mother is all about studying. The basics are crucial according to her, which she keeps reminding me, even though I pull her leg asking her whether she has any clue what I have been really studying in the last few years. Now she doesn't interfere much with my course studies, except to constantly goad me to do well, and to express sympathy. During my school years, she taught me the basics of maths, science and Hindi. The other two subjects, English and social science, were papa's responsibility.

My mother keeps claiming that whatever I am now is the result of the basics that she had fed in me through the early years. Maybe she is right. She now constantly eggs me on to complete my graduation. She wanted me to become an IAS officer or an engineer, and wishes to see me in formal attire going to an office. But now she either finds me in cricketing whites or in shorts and T-shirts, and most of her time goes in washing those dirty jerseys and arranging them properly at one place.

She is huge on sentimentality. Even today, whenever I am home, all three of us sleep together. Yes, I still sleep alongside my parents because that's the only way I sleep soundly. Maybe, it is because of my mom's caring touch.

Things have changed a lot over the years. Now I

shout at her not to disturb me while I am studying. But like a kid she comes to my room every ten minutes to kiss me. She doesn't always remember things these days but she is very insistent about knowing everything. She was hard on me when I screwed things up. Once I bullied one of my young schoolmates in the school bus, and his parents came to my house the same evening to complain. When they left, my mother was furious and gave me a real hard thrashing. Another time I was with a group of neighbourhood boys. We walked on a freshly laid rooftop and wrote something on the floor. Somehow my parents came to know about this and the way my mom came after me I thought she was going to kill me. There is no end to my mom's anger, and it is very difficult to pacify her. But she hardly raises her hand on me any more—those lovely days are gone.

My mom is also my best friend. I have never hidden anything from her. Believe me, 'everything' means 'everything'. She has a nice way of handling relationships. When I get into emotional troubles, she is the only person who can get me out of such situations. She does it in a very judicious way. She has always made correct predictions about the people around me. She understands human nature well and comes up with realistic solutions that would help me in the long run. Many of my friends come to her for advice, especially to overcome the blues of love. I have been lucky enough to be cautioned and guided by her. You need such a person when you are a vulnerable teenager, and especially because of my cricketing life.

I can't ever thank my mom enough for what she has done for me. The feeling is beyond any words.

Love you, mom!

My father, Bharat Chand Thakur

'*Papa kahte hain bada naam karega, beta hamara aisa kaam karega . . .*': that song from the movie *Qayamat Se Qayamat Tak* reminds me of my father. I am just a traveller walking along the path he has shown me. Plants grow when they get abundant light, from the sun. And my source, my guide, my sun has been my father. His quiet and effective way of dealing with all kinds of situations has been instrumental in shaping me. He is not someone who is boastful and with a loud mouth. He has quietly and carefully guided me using his own unique methods without my even noticing it.

My father used to take me to swimming practice on his Kinetic Honda at 5.30 in the morning and then he

12 May '05

On Your Maiden Century

Dear son,

I am sitting in the class at Jamia. But I am not able to concentrate as I just came to know about your century during the break.

Congratulations! At last you got what you were striving for a long. Today's century has proved that you have full potential of a good batsman at-opening position. You must carry on from here and be more consistent and reliable for the team.

Earlier in the morning, it was a great feeling to see today's perfect ground settings. A very big and lush green (Madan Lal Cricket Academy ground, Siri Fort), what you needed. I had an intuition in the morning, when I came to drop you there, that today was going to be your day.

So how you reached to your maiden century should be a great tale to be told. Ups and downs of the innings, how did you manage with different partners? You should write in detail. You should also write about your shortcomings, other feelings and reactions of your innings.

I missed the scene when you would have waved your bat on completion of your century 🙂 what were your thoughts at that moment? To whom you are dedicating this century?

Congratulations once again!
Wishing you great future!
Have fun today! 😊

Papa

**Dad Bharat Chand Thakur's letter to his son
on his first-ever century.**

would come back home and leave for his own school. He would come back from school in the afternoon and then take me to the National Stadium for practice. He would wait there in the hot sun till the practice was over and then bring me back home. Those were memorable days. I would be so tired by school and practice that I would fall asleep sitting behind him on the scooter. So to stop me from doing that, he would make me talk or cut jokes. Sometimes passing drivers would tell him that I have fallen asleep behind him. And then he would not stop talking to me till we reached home. Papa, the Kinetic Honda and I were close friends for a very long time. Sometimes, he used to take me and another player, with kits of course, on his scooter to faraway grounds for matches. I never missed a single day of practice because of his commitment towards me. He had reserved that time only for me. This routine continued for three to four years till I grew up enough to travel independently, in buses and the metro.

My father's priorities were very clear since my childhood. He wanted to build a strong foundation for my life and career; in doing so, he missed out on his own career and ambitions. The biggest quality that I have seen in him and learned from is that of being patient.

One thing for which I really thank dad is his deliberate emphasis on me writing a diary. I started keeping a diary when I began forming sentences in Hindi and English. When I look at those early childhood diaries, I feel very happy. My father would give me a topic to write on and then he would check and correct it. He would make me write down the names of all the books I have read and make me review them. That habit is still there with me, and I have been able to write this book because of my memory bank: my diaries. Through those diaries anybody can watch my life unfold day by day. I am someone who is excited by all sorts of dreams—nothing is enough for me. It intrigues me to think that I can add another trait to my identity: Unmukt Chand, cricketer and writer. And both are possible because of the inspiration and encouragement of my father.

My father is an avid reader and collector of books, newspapers and magazines, a bibliophile by nature. He gets hold of every article he can that relates to cricket, leadership and personality development, and then sends them to me. I have a handful of files with articles on various aspects of cricket, especially from the ESPN Cricinfo website and weekly columns in the newspapers by Harsha Bhogle and other experts.

I still have a paper clipping of young Cheteshwar Pujara when he had hit a triple century early on in his cricketing career; my dad had stuck that in my diary to motivate me. He made me read the book *What Sport Tells Us About Life* by Ed Smith very early. All this has helped me to interact with senior cricketers, coaches and other people, and also lead my team in the World Cup. This has also given me a lot of confidence in public speaking. You can always find a book, my diary and a dictionary in my bag.

My dad also pushed me hard to study, just like my mom! I still manage decent marks, even after studying just at the last hour. People say I don't need to be serious about studies any more, but I don't know why, I know I will always be studying religiously even for my semester exams in college. I am like this because my parents have made me like this. Dad teaches economics, and I was solely dependent on him for this subject in school and college as I could not attend classes there.

My dad is not materialistic at all. He is more than happy with what he has. Money has never been his driving force. He has rarely given me any expensive gifts on my birthday; his gift would be a good book. I am proud of my huge library with so many books on cricket, leadership, and some good autobiographies.

Even when I came back after winning the World Cup, my dad gave me a book: *Beyond A Boundary* by C.L.R. James. Though I must confess I didn't understand that book much. But I will, for sure, read it again once I have some grey hair. Dad's passion for books is so strong that he made me bring him a book *The Art of Cricket* by Don Bradman from Australia (from the Bradman Museum) when I was just twelve and touring with Bedi sir.

My dad has been so much involved with my cricket that he would go through all the statistics, like how many left-handed players the opposition has and the records of its bowlers and batsmen, and pass them on to me. He has maintained a file with all my newspaper clippings since my childhood and preserved all the videos and photographs of my cricketing career. He also sends me motivational, introspective messages that have helped me a lot. They have given me a higher level of understanding of certain things. His long messages help me see things that otherwise would have gone above my head. That constant eye always gazing over me has shown me the right direction, helped me avoid accidents, and made sure that I didn't get distracted. He has his own vision, and I rely so much on it. He always opens the doors to opportunities, doors that could lead me to glory and 'the path of victory'. He is my very old buddy. He has managed my whole life meticulously. His shadow always follows me and I am sure I won't let his efforts go waste.

My uncle, Sunder Chand Thakur

The biggest gift I was born with is my chachu (uncle). He is the one who has made everything happen, transformed ideas into reality. He is an ex-army man and now the editor of *Navbharat Times*, Mumbai. He is also a renowned Hindi poet and novelist. He has recently written a novel, *Patthar Per Doob*, and he is after me to read it—I hope I will soon. At the age of forty-two, he ran the Mumbai marathon two years ago and now he is a regular marathon runner. There is an interesting story behind his running the marathon.

It was my second Ranji season for Delhi and I was very hopeful of getting enough runs under my belt. Both of us love challenges. Though he is a person who commits first and then acts, I generally prefer doing things the other way round—act first and only then talk about it. So he challenged me. He said, 'You score 1000 runs in the Ranji season and I will run the full marathon.' It sounded interesting, so I took the deal. And, even though I didn't manage to get 1000 runs, he kept his side of the deal comfortably. Mind you, running a full marathon needs courage, practice and mental strength. And that chachu has in abundance. He is a man who just cannot accept defeat. A great motivator, he can motivate a donkey to be a lion. One of the reasons that he has kept himself so physically fit is to train me. Until just a few years ago he would challenge me to 100 m sprints. His mental strength is amazing. Even today, whenever he is in Delhi, he will take me to the basement and bowl at me (with a wet tennis ball) for hours.

My early memories of him go back to the time when I started playing cricket. Those days we lived as a joint family. He would take me for long runs. He would plan my whole routine and involve himself in everything I had to do. There used to be long fitness sessions. He would pay attention to everything—how I talk, walk, what I wear ... It is because of his persistence that I no longer stand with one of my legs bent. He just used to hate it. 'Only donkeys stand on one leg,' he would say and kick me even in public. Such is his army discipline.

Chachu has always drilled into me the importance of routine. He still sends me a daily planner that I should follow. His favourite line is: 'How can you waste something as precious as time? There is so much to do in life, so much to learn, to read, to explore; work on personality development!' He hates it when I tell him that I am getting bored. 'Only fools and aimless people get bored. How can you have so much time to do so?' he retorts.

Chachu has taught me so many things. He likes to say, 'Do whatever you are doing in the best possible way of doing it.' Now I use his teachings to guide others. All his teaching and training have become a part of me, so much so that I have become his alter ego. We speak to each other at least thrice a day. It does not matter where I am, in India or abroad, I don't remember a single day of my conscious life when we have not spoken. Our talks are always constructive and goal oriented. Now I realize that he has made me a sort of workaholic. Things that seemed difficult to me he has made them look easier. He has always believed in pushing the limits and I have really been trying to do that. Whatever he learns, he passes it on to me. For the last few months he has been pushing me to begin my day with a proper plan of what I will be doing. Initially, I had reservations about it as I did not feel it necessary to write things down. But when I actually started doing it, I found it really made me more focused and saved me precious time. It took away all my confusion and indecisiveness. He is trying to make me a real professional.

All his instructions and lectures are part of my system now, and they help me to react well under any circumstance. He has taught me to be positive, to stay away from things that give you negative vibes. Another mantra that he has given me is, 'whatever happens, happens for the best'. Cricket is a game where you go through ups and downs; the downs especially are frequent. You need to learn to deal with them. I am lucky that I have my uncle with me. It just takes a phone call and there he is churning out the best of motivational speeches and pushing away all negative thoughts.

My uncle does not limit himself to cricket. Obviously, it is the most talked about thing between us, but we discuss many more things. As he always tells me, life is much more than cricket. My uncle's interests have been diverse. He wants me to play for the country and play like a champion, but he also wants me to be an equally known figure outside cricketing circles—I should be able to speak knowledgeably to masters of other fields, or on issues apart from cricket. He wants to see me delivering speeches to the students of IIM one day on topics like leadership, time management, etc. His emphasis has always been on multi-dimensional growth. He wants me to do so many things. I am trying my best to meet his expectations. One last thing that he pushes me to do is to give back to society. I hope someday I will be in a position to really do that, though I have started doing it in whatever little ways I can right now.

You must by now have understood how this chacha–bhatija (uncle–nephew) jodi works. Yeah! We are always working together, setting new goals, and discussing ways to achieve them. As he tells me quite often, the encouragement and motivation is flowing from both sides now. My success inspires him and, in turn, he inspires me to achieve bigger success.

Chachu is also my 3 a.m. friend. I tell him everything that's happening on and off the field. He knows me better than I know myself. I have shared literally everything under the sun with him—I think that's a rare kind of relationship, especially within a family. We form a formidable pair and I'm sure our partnership is going to rock. We respect and trust each other, and I am sure we will together achieve greater heights. My chachu is my god, my guru and my real hero.

My coach, Sanjay Bhardwaj

There is always one person in your life who is not family but eventually becomes so close that you can trust him, fall back upon him, speak your heart out to him and learn from him. Talking to this person always makes you feel good, surrounded as he is by an air of calm and positivity. These feelings are so infectious that they cling to you as well and you feel confident about yourself. The person I am talking about here is none other than my coach, Sanjay sir.

Sanjay sir is not an unknown figure in the cricketing circle; he has coached Gautam Gambhir and Amit Mishra too. He has produced innumerable domestic players who have done great jobs for their states. He has been coaching cricketers for the last fifteen to twenty years and has a vast knowledge of the game. His passion for cricket made him travel from Rohtak in Haryana to Bharat Nagar, Delhi, every day until he produced a couple of international players, and settled near the ground itself.

Sanjay sir is a great human being and a man with a very big heart. He doesn't worry too much about the future and believes in his work. According to him, the fight should be to master your field; then the future will take care of itself. If you work hard with a clear mindset, god automatically puts everything in place and opens up new doors, he would say.

I love his simplicity and his inquisitiveness. For him, nothing is above cricket. Though his financial state is not stable, he still does everything and anything for his pupils. He has created a wonderful atmosphere in Bharat Nagar for cricketers to learn and grow. He could have easily earned a lot of money and led a comfortable life, but his focus has always been on improving us. For him, our success is his success. That's why he lives in the same way as he did ten years ago. He doesn't want to change because it might distract him and make him lazy. This is one of the things about him that has really impressed me.

Sir always tells me that he is the lucky one, because I came to him out of nowhere like a gift from god. That is his greatness, his humility. People don't generally say such things. Today, coaches fight to claim that they are the ones who coached so and so player, even if in reality that player had just a few practice sessions under them. But Sanjay sir is different. He believes in giving, not taking. His unselfish approach to life is something that puts him ahead of everyone. My love and respect for him has increased manifold over the years.

I have always wondered why there are pilgrimage centres all around. Why can't people do puja at their own home? What is so different about these places that people feel very close to god there? Now I get it. The Bharat Nagar ground has some special thing about it, in its soil, that makes learning easier. It's a pilgrimage centre for cricket students. It's a temple for me where I get so much peace and so many positive vibes. Batting in the nets under the supervision of Sanjay sir is like going through a meditation session.

And to tell you the truth, it's not just a club; it's also a home for children who have come from various parts of the country. Sir has made rooms for them to stay there. There is a cook who makes food for them. Trust me, you will not find these facilities anywhere in the country. And mind you, he doesn't charge for this. There are so many poor children living there. He, in fact, spends from his own pocket for their travel and daily needs. There is no one to sponsor tournament fees. He understands the importance of exposure through matches, therefore he himself pays the fee.

I always wonder where he finds the strength to give so much when he himself is not financially secure. He doesn't run a business. He has his family to support too. But I have never seen any signs of worry on his face. This is the power of belief and giving. If you believe in something so strongly, then everything automatically falls into place. He believes in hard work and is a cricket freak. His love for me is unique. I am his blue-eyed boy. He has bet very high stakes on me.

Sanjay sir is one of those people who share their experiences and love to talk to me about life. His main aim is to make me a great human being first—being a great cricketer will follow. He understands the importance of other things in life apart from cricket. He believes that the more positive you stay, the happier you become. It is a state of mind and one should remain calm in every situation. His guidance and tips have brought a sea change to my batting and my outlook towards life. Whether I am away at the NCA or touring some other country, he has always brought me peace by talking to me over the phone. I always call him before matches to get the last 'knockout punch' from him and he sends me to the battlefield with his blessings. His two-minute pep talk gives me a boost and fills me with confidence.

People don't understand the hard work that goes on behind the scenes in the making of a player. Each and every move I make on the ground is a result of the constant guidance of my mentors. Pressure disappears when I close my eyes and visualize my mentors standing in front of me and telling me to go and conquer the world. 'Come on, son, nothing can stop you now. We are with you.' I really feel lucky to have such a family. I can only promise them that I will achieve goals worth all their sweat.

Acknowledgements

There are many noble souls out there who have helped me become the person that I am; they have shaped my personality, my life, and of course my cricketing sense. My sincere gratitude to all of them.

It would have been impossible to write this book without the wholehearted support of my family, friends and well-wishers. I wish to thank each one of them:

My uncle Sunder Chand Thakur for conceiving the idea of this book much before the Under-19 World Cup, and then constantly pushing me to complete it.

My father Bharat Chand Thakur for typing out the entire manuscript, while at times getting irritated by the illegible handwriting in my diaries. His patience has ultimately paid off. And all the clippings that he had collected over the years—ever since my childhood days—came in very handy in putting this book together.

Joseph Mathai uncle and Snehlata aunty for hand-holding me and taking me through the secrets of writing a book; the discussions I had with them have proved to be invaluable.

Lekhasri Samantsinghar aunty for going through the entire draft patiently, correcting the text and giving her precious feedback.

Varun Chopra and Gagan Jain of Medallin Sports for coordinating with the publisher, and Manish Patankar for helping me with the data.

Ameya Nagarajan, my editor with Penguin, for transforming raw writing into a presentable work; Shanuj V.C., another editor, for going through the proofs, polishing it, and giving it the final touch.

Ashok Pandey uncle for always enriching me with books, films and ideas since my childhood.

Last but not least, my mother Rajeshwari Chand, who has been the real source of my energy in whatever I do.

My very special thanks also goes to Sir Vivian Richards, Sachin Tendulkar, V.V.S. Laxman and Rahul Dravid for reading the manuscript and sparing the time to offer me words of wisdom and encouragement.